Eyewitnesses
To American
Jewish History

Edited by

AZRIEL EISENBERG

UNION OF AMERICAN HEBREW CONGREGATIONS · New York

Sonnets.

I.

The New Colossus.

Not like the brazen giant of Greek fame,
With conquering limbs astride from land to land;
Here at our sea-washed, sunset gates shall stand
A mighty woman with a torch, whose flame
Is the imprisoned lightning, and her name
Mother of Exiles. From her beacon-hand
Glows world-wide welcome; her mild eyes command
The air-bridged harbor that twin cities frame.

"Keep, ancient lands, your storied pomp!" cries she
With silent lips. "Give me your tired, your poor,
Your huddled masses yearning to breathe free,
The wretched refuse of your teeming shore.
Send these, the homeless, tempest-tost to me,
I lift my lamp beside the golden door!"

1883.

(Written in aid of Bartholdi Pedestal Fund.)

EYEWITNESSES TO AMERICAN JEWISH HISTORY

A History of American Jewry

PART III·The Eastern European Immigration·1881-1920

To
DR. ABRAHAM P. GANNES
Esteemed Co-worker and Friend

CONTENTS

FOREWORD

From 1881-1882—the outbreak of the Russian pogroms and the enactment of the so-called May Laws of 1882 which herded Jews into the ghettos of the Pale—to World War I in 1914, some 200,000 Jews left East Europe for America.

Quantitatively and qualitatively, the Eastern European immigration wave molded the American Jewish community. The immigrants brought with them a rich and colorful cultural heritage which shaped Jewish life: orthodoxy, conservatism, socialism, unionism; diverse Zionist ideologies, political, religious, cultural, and labor; Yiddish literary creativity such as is seen in the press and the theater; Hebrew; Jewish scholarship; and the romance of Chasidism and its offshoots in music, art, and dance. These themes form Part III and will overflow into Part IV, the final section of this work, which treats of the emergence of what may be called the "American Jew."

I am beholden to Mrs. Hannah Grad Goodman for editing the introductions and condensing many of the selections; also for her contribution of selection 26 (Lotta Levensohn Recounts the Beginnings of Hadassah). I am also pleased to acknowledge my thanks to Sima M. Horowitz, librarian for the American Jewish Committee; Sylvia Landress, librarian of the Zionist library of the Jewish Agency; Philip Miller, librarian at Hebrew Union College-Jewish Institute of Religion; Dr. Leonard Gold, librarian of the Jewish Room of the New York Public Library; and their staffs for the many courtesies extended to me during my research.

I am grateful to Rabbi Daniel Syme, director of the Commission on Jewish Education; to Mr. Ralph Davis and his associates, Mrs. Josette Knight, Mrs. Annette Abramson, and Mrs. Esther Fried Africk, for their help in seeing the book through to publication; and to Mrs. Bernice Linder who typed the manuscript.

I am thankful to the authors and publishers of the books who granted me permission to reprint the selections and to the agencies which permitted me to reproduce the illustrations. Specific acknowledgments are made following each selection and illustration.

Finally, my eternal gratitude to my wife who has borne with me in my preoccupation with writing over these many years. She has also proofread with her usual meticulous care.

A.E.

Eyewitnesses
To American
Jewish History

The Statue of Liberty, by French sculptor Frederic Auguste Bartholdi, was presented to the United States by the French government, July 4, 1884. Welcoming immigrants to New York harbor,
the statue symbolizes our national ideals. (American Jewish
Archives)

Emma Lazarus's famous sonnet was inscribed at the base of the
statue in 1903. In her own handwriting, the sonnet appears on the
title page. (American Jewish Historical Society)

A LABOR LEADER Recalls
the Sudden Rise and Fall
of the First Cloakmakers' Union
in New York, 1881

Tailoring is one of the world's oldest trades. As soon as Adam and Eve ate of the apple and became uncomfortable because of their nakedness, they sewed fig leaves together and made themselves aprons.

Most of the early American garment manufacturers were German Jews, men and women, who immigrated to the United States after the European revolutions of 1848. With the invention (1880) of the electric cutting knife, which cut six to eight sheets of cloth at one time, and the sewing machine, whose treadle was propelled like a bicycle by the leg of the operator, men replaced women because of their superior physical strength. Operators were now recruited largely from the immigrant Russian and Polish Jews, and three-fourths of the clothing workers, almost all men, were concentrated in New York City.

The sewing and pressing of the garments were farmed out by the manufacturers to special contractors. Prices fluctuated depending on the supply of labor and the competition among the sweatshops. According to statistics cited in *Tailor's Progress* by Benjamin Stolberg (Doubleday Doran, 1944), in 1880 there were 25,192 workers in 562 shops; by 1890 there were 39,149 in 1,224. The contractor was usually an individual who had arrived in America a little earlier than the others, rented an "apartment," and attracted newcomers from his home town to work for him. Often the workers boarded and lodged with the family. The children helped in various small chores and the wife assisted in finishing off the product. In the eighties wages ranged from seven to fifteen dollars per week for men and about half of this amount for women. The workers put in from twelve to sixteen hours per day. Contractors were powerless to pay higher wages unless the manufacturers increased payments to them. As a result, workers often lived on the verge of poverty. For them, America was hardly a land of plenty.

"Each marcher carried a broomstick, symbolizing the act of sweeping out the foul sweatshops from our midst"

SHORTLY AFTER PASSOVER, I stood lost in thought at the corner of Essex and Hester Streets, popularly known as the *chazer mark*, "pig market," which was a "labor exchange" where job hunters and contractors sought each other out. Suddenly a man stopped and began questioning me. "Are you a cloakmaker?" to which I replied "No." "Maybe you are a presser?" Again, "No." He persisted, "Would you like to learn to become a presser?"

I had arrived nine months ago without a trade. I had tried various jobs like peddling matches, baking *matzot*, and working as a barber. When I heard the offer I eagerly assented.

Pressing clothes was regarded as one of the more desirable trades at that time. Frequently, at the height of the season, contractors clustered around Castle Garden [the place of landing in New York harbor from 1855 to 1890] and snatched the immigrants as soon as they descended from the gangplank. And, if the newcomers had had experience in the needle trade, the bosses fought over them like prizes.

Happy at my good luck, I began asking for details, when I quickly struck a snag. My prospective employer asked me if I possessed the required fee of five dollars to pay for learning the job. (In those days all learners had to pay from $5 [for a presser] to $10 [for an operator] to become an apprentice.) Five dollars was beyond my reach. I thought quickly and replied, "I shall be glad to pay the $5 in weekly installments from my wages."

My lucky star was with me. After arguing back and forth, he agreed. I was launched in my new occupation. Little did I know that it would lead to my life's commitment in the field of labor relations.

Pressing was a simple operation and anyone could master it within a week. Even though I soon became an experienced presser, I had to serve four weeks without pay and then begin to pay out my weekly installments. There were other "hurdles" that a *greener* had to overcome. During my month's apprenticeship I also underwent a period of "hazing" (like a college freshman). I had to humble myself before the old-timers, jump to obey their requests, and in general to be servile to my "superiors" until I made it. This was the "system" and no one dared to challenge it.

None of us had any notion of unionizing to better our conditions. By mere chance we heard about workers organizing to demand better wages and that they stopped work when refused. This action was called "to strike." One day we learned that longshoremen, who loaded and unloaded baggage and crates on and off ships at the waterfront, had gone on strike. The shipowners sent agents to Hester and Market Streets to engage replacements. They promised us 40 cents per hour and steady work. Our *chevrah* knew nothing about the daily happenings since there were no Yiddish papers at the time and they could not read English. They jumped at the offer, abandoned their machines, and off they went to the docks. They had no idea about the risks they were taking. Every morning they were collected in groups at specified locations and delivered to the docks. It did not take long for the Irish strikers to beat up some of the strikebreakers; a number had to be hospitalized. The "scabs" quickly returned to their sewing machines.

But the incident taught us a lesson: When workers unite they can improve their lot and earn better wages. We began to discuss plans to force the issue with our employers.

In the ready-made garment industry there were two establishments, the "outside" shops where we worked and the "inside"

shops which were located on Broadway. The former were in the
hands of people who were the contractors. The latter were com-
prised of mostly German Jews whose firms were complete with
designers, cutters (who cut the garments for us to sew), furnished
show rooms, sales rooms, and offices. We were not aware of this
arrangement. We were intimidated from applying for jobs on
Broadway because we knew no English, we were more comfortable with our *landsleit*, and, most importantly, we would have
had to desecrate the Sabbath; working on the Sabbath day was
unthinkable.

One day a contractor, in a quarrel with a worker, slapped his
face. In protest against this abusive behavior the workers dropped
what they were doing and walked out in anger. They rented a
room at 165 East Broadway and met to consider what action to
take. After a long harangue, a proposal was made that we issue
a call for a general strike. The response to the proposal was un-
expectedly favorable. About 5,000 workers walked out on strike.

Extemporaneously we elected two operators and two pressers
as our leaders and spokesmen. One of the operators was nicknamed Baruch "Shiker" (drunkard), the fastest worker in the
industry. On payday, contractors would vie with each other to
inveigle him to work in their shops by plying him with liquor.

Baruch Shiker often played pranks on his fellow workers. Once
he stole into the shop after closing hours and spent all night in
sewing the garments which had been delivered in a bundle for
us to work on the next day. He repacked them in the bundle and
left the shop before the men reported to work. When the men
arrived and found the garments all sewn, they were furious at
Baruch who rollicked in laughter. He was admired for his abilities
as a jolly good fellow and as a public speaker. When he arose to
speak, everyone listened to him with fond respect. He asked for
and won the support of his fellow workers, and all resolved as one
to fight to the end.

Fortunately, a group of Russian Jewish intellectuals and students joined our cause. They were young socialists who agitated
to wipe out the shame of the sweatshops and the evils of the

A young child carrying work to be done at home. (American Jewish Archives)

A typical sweatshop on New York City's Lower East Side. (American Jewish Archives)

contract system. At one of our meetings, one of them moved that we organize into a union and persist in persuading all workers to join. The dues were set initially at 50 cents a month. As the crowds began to mill around the table to pay their dues, the price began to rise until it reached $2. On the second day it was set at $5 per month.

Enthusiasm was high. The strike lasted three weeks and the contractors gave in. The men were jubilant and resolved to celebrate their victory with a parade. Each marcher carried a broomstick, symbolizing the act of sweeping out the foul sweatshops from our midst. The press publicized the bizarre event and we were applauded far and wide.

But, alas, the morning after the victory march when we assembled in our respective Broadway firms, the employees refused to work under the same roof with us. We were the *"greeners"* and they the "Americans." The contractors and their employers were pleased at this development and politely suggested that we return to our East Side shops. Having lost three weeks' pay and with Passover nigh, we swallowed our pride and shamefacedly went back where we came from. The union soon dissolved; its meager funds were dissipated and the cloakmakers' union died aborning.

Translated from the Yiddish by the editor

From *The Cloakmakers and Their Unions: Memoirs,*
by Abraham Rosenberg, Cloak Operators Union Local One,
New York, 1920, pp. 3–9

AN IMMIGRANT Reports on the Russian Jewish Refugees in Western Canada, 1882

The vicious Russian pogroms of 1881 aroused loathing and condemnation in England and the United States, resulting in protests and demonstrations. In addition, leaders throughout the world were revolted by the May Laws of 1882 which restricted Jews to a specified geographic area, the Pale of Settlement, prohibiting their living or acquiring property outside of that area.

In London, for example, the sponsors of protest demonstrations included outstanding personalities like Charles Darwin, Robert Browning, Matthew Arnold, James Bryce, and Cardinal Manning. Emergency committees were formed to help the victims who had fled Russia and inundated the port cities of Europe. The London committee, with the humanitarian aid of British and Canadian authorities, arranged for the migration of the victims to the open prairies of western Canada.

The first immigrants began to arrive in Winnipeg, Manitoba, in May, 1882, which was then populated by a total of about 7,000 people. On the whole, the newcomers were book-minded, learned in Hebrew, and unaccustomed to hard labor.

Life was difficult. At first they were housed in ramshackle wooden barracks. Prices were very high (potatoes cost five dollars a bushel) and newcomers were given only half a potato each per meal. They were mobilized to work at building railroad tracks, hewing stones, digging ditches, and other activities for which they were physically unprepared. Their first experiences are reflected in a letter, quoted below, sent by one of the immigrants to the Russian Hebrew newspaper *Hamelitz* (*The Advocate*), the central organ of Russian Jewry.

Slowly, the despairing mood began to abate, as we see in his second letter three months later, on September 17, 1882.

By the end of 1882, the newcomers organized their first congregation, B'nai Israel (Sons of Israel) and, a few months later, Ezrath Ahim (Brotherly Help). They "made" it.

"We had not been accustomed to perform such hard labor."

[June, 1882]

I LL-FATED we were from the very first night that we arrived here. All day long we did neither eat nor drink, simply because we had not a cent to buy anything with. Hungry and thirsty we lay on the floor of our sheltering home, and the progeny of the Pharaoh's third plague (lice) preyed upon us. Thus we were tormented all night, and with the rise of dawn we hastened to work in order to earn the means to buy bread for our families. Before our limbs had as yet rested from our protracted and wearisome journey . . . we had to haul heavy sacks of wheat from the steamer into the sheds. . . . We had not been accustomed to perform such hard labor. Sixty men we are here, all learned and educated Jews; all are well versed in Hebrew and many of us also in some European language. We wanted to come here in order to honestly earn our livelihood in a land where we would not be exposed to the mockery and ridicule of our Gentile neighbours because of our faith and looks. We were exiled to a desert. Even such work as chopping wood, hewing stone, or digging soil is not to be found, and the cost of living, to boot, is extremely high here.

One does not so much as see the shadow of a committee that would come to the aid of the wretched immigrant during the first days of his stay in this country. We shall perish from hunger and cold which here reaches 40 degrees below zero during the winter. What is worse still is that there are very few regularly built houses. There are only canvas tents, in which we, too, live. . . . Thousands of Jews have been sent to desert regions, with an unbearable climate, where they are compelled to work at hard labor even on Saturdays and holidays in order to earn the barest livelihood constructing railways. . . . They must eat stale and *trefah* [nonkosher] meat so as to have the necessary strength to carry on their backs the heavy loads, or to do the pick and shovel work. . . .

It is evident that under such circumstances no one can think of reading a newspaper or a book. . . . Nor have we enough time to do our daily prayers. We come home at night and, wearied and exhausted, sleep overtakes us before we have even eaten. We shall all perish here and not have so much as a Jewish burial. The child of an immigrant died here today and there is no burial ground for it. . . .

*   *   *   *   *

"*. . . Away from the city and from human society, they still remember the God of their ancestors.*"

September 17, 1882

I KNOW that my first letter was a source of pain to many of our people. Perhaps I have somewhat exaggerated. . . . The situation has, however, thank God, partly improved. We have gradually become inured to our hard labours, whether they be the construction of some new railway lines, the carrying of mortar and cement for the erection of some new buildings, or the laying of sewers in the streets of Winnipeg and similar other work. We are paid from $2.50 to $3.00 per day and we have found favour with our employers. (The New York and Winnipeg newspapers have nothing but words of praise for the Jewish refugees in Canada and compare us favourably with those of our brethren who have gone to the United States. . . .)

Here in this new country, even the cultured and well-bred

among us have soon discarded their starched shirts and lacquered shoes and have set themselves to work. . . . One is grieved, however, with things educational and spiritual, which are growing worse daily. Our children wander recklessly about the streets and humiliate us in the eyes of our neighbours. None of us is concerned with engaging teachers for them to give them a religious education or otherwise to establish some school for them. . . .

. . . *Rosh Hashanah* was celebrated in our tents near the railway station, some forty miles from Winnipeg. Each of us donated three dollars and thus we collected the sum of one hundred dollars which we have sent to New York, ordering a *Sefer Torah* and a *shofar*. We all stopped from work and gathered in a large tent and poured out our hearts in prayers, before God, during the Day of Atonement. The Christian inhabitants, who had never seen nor heard the like before, collected in groups without and admiringly said: "Away from the city and from human society, they still remember the God of their ancestors."

From *History of the Jews in Canada*, Vol. I,
by Benjamin G. Sack, Canadian Jewish Congress,
1945, pp. 185–188

JUDAH DAVID EISENSTEIN
Reports on a Jewish Colony in Vineland, New Jersey, 1882

The year 1881 was a decisive time in Jewish history. In the spring of that year, pogroms broke out in more than 160 Russian towns and villages, bringing destruction and devastation to their Jewish inhabitants.

It was clearly time to leave Eastern Europe, and "emigration" became the rallying cry of Jews everywhere. For the great majority, emigration was a matter of physical survival. For others, however, especially students and intellectuals, leaving Eastern Europe was seen as the first step in realizing high ideals.

The *Bilu* groups were early pioneers, for example, who settled as agriculturists in Palestine. (*Bilu* is an acronym for *bet Yaakov lechu venelchah,* "O house of Jacob, come ye, and let us walk. . . ," from Isaiah 2:5.) They were followed by successive waves of *chalutzim* who laid the groundwork for the modern State of Israel and who later became part of the Zionist movement. A second group, the Bundists were Jewish socialists who joined the Russian socialist and revolutionary parties fighting the czarist regime, attempting to force political reforms. (The *Bund* or Union, the movement whose members were called Bundists, is an abbreviation for the General Federation of Jewish Workers in Lithuania, Poland, and Russia.) Finally, there was the *Am Olam* (Eternal People or World People) movement. It was organized in Odessa after the pogroms of May 3–5, 1881. Its adherents strove to "normalize" Jewish life in a free America, returning to the soil and creating a society based on equality and self-fulfillment.

Thus, many groups of Jews wanted to leave Eastern

Europe, and influential Jewish philanthropists throughout the world helped them to find new homes. One such individual was the world renowned railroad builder and financier, Baron Maurice de Hirsch (1831–96). In 1887, after he had lost his only son, he declared, "My son I have lost, but not my heir. Humanity is my heir." And indeed it was. Baron de Hirsch gave generously of himself and his millions to resettle his people in colonies like the one described in the selection by Judah David Eisenstein.

Judah David Eisenstein (1854–1956) was a prominent American author and scholar who edited the first Hebrew encyclopedia (published in ten volumes) as well as outstanding anthologies on Jewish travel literature, *Midrash*, and disputations between Jewish and Christian scholars. He contributed to the *Jewish Encyclopedia* and left a deep imprint on Hebrew literature in America. He had come to New York in 1872 and was a correspondent for *Hamelitz*. Eisenstein's report on the colony which was established by the Hebrew Emigrant Aid Society in Vineland, New Jersey, was carried in the *New York World*, July 2, 1882.

"All are in good spirits as we see them."

AFTER I HAD WALKED four miles . . . I turned right on a new road which was full of winding paths and obstacles, piles of sand and trunks of trees that had been cut down. Then one comes near to the plateau on which the colony is situated so beautifully. When you are within a quarter of a mile of the colony there appears before your eyes a flagpole at the top of the mountain. On it flies the flag of the United States . . . under whose protection these colonists . . . find security. Less than two months have passed since the colony was founded in the midst of the woods. . . . The virgin soil which is evident to all bears witness that, on this new land which was just opened for development, there will be a permanent settlement.

Five long buildings of the same height were built across from one another. They are wooden buildings made of cut logs, plain and nice looking even though not painted. It was midday when I arrived there. The men, women, and children were gathered all around the houses. Some were sitting alongside of the houses and relaxing in the shade, some were reclining or standing. . . . Others were drawing water . . . amongst whom there were thirty or forty women. Fifty or sixty children were romping like young sheep in the pastures. The children all looked healthy, half-dressed or fully dressed, beautiful and nodding babes, not washed, powdered, or rouged, but attractive. Every person who met me as I passed by lifted his hand to his hat and tipped it as a sign of respect and greeted me. . . .

I came into the administrative office and met Mr. Sternberger [the colony superintendent], his wife, and [his] secretary who were helping him measure and cut strips of cotton cloth patterned for clothes which were to be distributed to each family, according to the size of the family, for coats, shirts, and dresses, etc.

After I told him the purpose of my visit, he welcomed me and told me that these garments are given to each person. He said, "I tell them privately, although it is not really true, that I am not giving this cloth to them as a gift, rather that I am lending it to them until they will be able to support themselves, so that they may not be humiliated."

In the meantime, a bell announced time for lunch and about 200 or 300 people, men, women, and children, hastened quietly to the dining room. Each one was doled out a portion of chicken soup, broth, and boiled meat. . . .

There were no sweets, no fats, but good food. . . . The meat is brought daily from Philadelphia from a kosher slaughter house. It is absolutely kosher. When they sat down to eat I was able to observe these people as much as I wished. They were much healthier looking than the new immigrants which one sees in

New York. Their bodies looked strong. Many were fine looking people. They were from five feet eight inches to five feet eleven inches in height. . . . While they were eating, they sat dressed in clothes like farmers and toilers of the soil at the time of work. The women were dressed up, but their garbs were plain and clean, dressed like farmers' wives. . . . Most of them were healthy looking and attractive. Above all, the boys and girls looked healthy and well fed.

All the men know how to write and to read books written in their own language. Some of them also read and write Russian. All of them read Hebrew and are so well versed in their prayers that they know them by heart. Every day they pray three times a day, evening, morning, and afternoon, and on the Sabbath conduct longer services. They have no minister, rabbi, or ritual leader in their midst. One of the members of the group leads in the services also on the Sabbath. They refrain from all work on the Sabbath days, but on Sundays they go forth to their work. They know their history well and all the glories of their ancestors and the tribulations of the exile which are engraved on their hearts with an emery wheel. Therefore, they recognize the change for good which has transpired for them in escaping from the afflictions of their persecutors and pursuers and in coming to a land of peace where they can live with honor amongst people who have respect for their fellow men and consider this the first principle of life.

On the 4th of July the builders amongst them constructed gates and high domes on which they put stars. The women vied with one another in decorating them with green boughs and flowers and tied on flags of the nation in honor of this day in accordance with the law of the country. This was to teach the people about the birth of the Republic. Every American celebrated this holiday and sang patriotic songs with enthusiasm.

However, the question is will Isaac, Moshe, and Shlomo, even if they know their holidays, also know the ways of the farmer? Will they follow the ways of the farmer? Will they choose the cultivation of the soil in Vineland or will they follow the scent of the peddlers who have grown up in Bayard and Ludlow streets and work in the Bowery and Chatham streets?

More than one hundred souls lived under one roof, but the rooms were clean and clear of a speck of dirt. I walked through the passageways of each of the buildings and did not detect a whiff of any unpleasant odor. . . .

They went forth in groups to their work, each group had a leader and teacher . . . under the supervision of a director. When the bell sounded four o'clock in the morning they arose and went into the fields to work. If they were told to reap, they did so; to weed, they did so; to hoe, they did so. At six o'clock they returned for breakfast, after which they continued to work until nine o'clock. From nine until two in the afternoon they were free to be home, to rest, to change clothes. . . . When the two-o'clock bell rang, they returned to work until seven o'clock in the evening. One of the women showed me that she had learned how to milk the cows, but who will foretell what the younger generation will do.

Mr. Sternberger is a non-Jew, but he has been in close contact with Jewish people for many years. . . . He has stated voluntarily that he can prove to the world that the Jews are capable of becoming farmers in America. The greater question according to him is whether they are able to carry the burden of this work and not weaken either because of helplessness or impatience or slowness. Now it was proved that these people did their work for two continuous months without any fatigue or harm. All are in good spirits as we see them. Therefore, our hope is strengthened that the Committee in New York will allocate . . . tracts of land [to students] after they complete their studies by the end of the summer. Then they will be on their own. Mr. Sternberger is very confident that the Committee will not disappoint him. In the last report which he sent to the Executive Committee at the end of the past month, he wrote concerning his pupils that in his thirty years of experience he never had such diligent and attentive students as these and that they are all eagerly waiting to stand on their own feet and not to have to be dependent on the Committee. Some were beginning to grow impatient. At present they have nothing as the land, houses, cattle, vessels in the houses, agricultural implements, and utensils belong to the Committee of New York. The latter provides for all their needs including furnishings of the houses and clothes. There will be little income from this year's harvest as the soil which is tilled for the first year does not yield much. They are at present poor and beggarly.

Judah David Eisenstein

From the *New York World,* July 2, 1882,
as quoted in *American Jewish Historical Quarterly,*
June, 1971

DAVID PHILIPSON Remembers the Early Religious Development of Reform Jewry, 1883–1888

David Philipson (1862–1949) was one of the pioneers of Reform Judaism. He lived through the exciting, turbulent, and creative years when the young movement was first making its presence felt and winning a place in the ranks of American Jewry.

As a thirteen-year-old Indiana boy he entered the Hebrew Union College in Cincinnati on October 3, 1875, one of twenty youths who took part in Isaac M. Wise's brave new experiment. Eight years later he was one of four young men ordained as rabbis in its first graduating class.

An American-born and American-trained rabbi, Dr. Philipson carried the banner of Reform Judaism into the eastern part of the United States. He was a participant in the famous 1885 Pittsburgh Conference of the Central Conference of American Rabbis which drew up the controversial Pittsburgh Platform. He helped create the Jewish Publication Society of America and held top offices in a number of organizations. Having worked intimately with some of the great figures of his time—Rabbi Isaac M. Wise, Dr. Kaufmann Kohler, Cyrus Adler, and Dr. Sabato Morais—he gives us illuminating glimpses of their characters and personalities.

"I have lived through many great moments, but never have I seen a company so exaltingly excited."

DURING the pioneer years, the Hebrew Union College was on trial. Isaac M. Wise was constantly conscious of this. . . . He therefore conceived the idea of bringing, at the close of each academic year, three examiners from various parts of the country . . . well-known rabbis and occasionally a layman versed in biblical and talmudic lore, such as Lewis N. Dembitz [uncle of the late Supreme Court Justice Louis Dembitz Brandeis] of Louisville, Ky. That Dembitz, one of the keenest legal minds in the country, was . . . very orthodox and therefore entirely unsympathetic to the Reform position made no difference. The contention of the founder always was that the College was an academic institution and had room for all shades of Jewish religious opinion and practice. His feeling was that, if scholars, no matter where their religious sympathies lay, would find the instruction . . . sound, this would form the finest recommendation . . . that the institution was eminently worthy of support. Therefore, he invited, not only men of the Reform school, but even the leading Orthodox rabbi of the country, Sabato Morais, of Mikveh Israel Congregation of Philadelphia.

Morais was uncompromisingly orthodox in his Jewish life and teaching. An intense man in every phase of his being, this rabbi of Italian birth created a profound impression on the student body. He joined with his fellow examiners in a laudatory report of . . . the College. In a few years, however, when the Reform policy of the institution became unmistakable, Morais headed a countermovement that eventuated in . . . the Jewish Theological Seminary of America in New York, a training school for Conservative rabbis . . . which became the "rival" of the Hebrew Union College.

There was room for this other institution . . . there have always been different parties in Judaism . . . conflicting opinions. The strength of Judaism has largely consisted in the fact that there was room for such differences. Reference need only be made to the famous dictum called forth by the conflicting pronouncements of the so-called schools of Hillel and Shammai . . . both were declared to be acceptable interpretations when it was stated, *Elu ve'elu divrei Elohim chayim*, "Both the declarations of the school of Hillel and the school of Shammai are the words of the living God." Real toleration can no further go. The Jewish Theological Seminary and the Hebrew Union College have served their purposes in Jewish religious endeavor, and today there exists an *entente cordiale.* . . .

Half a century and more ago . . . no one in his wildest dreams would have imagined that the day would ever come when a Reform rabbi would preach from the pulpit of Sabato Morais. And yet . . . in December, 1939, I occupied that famed pulpit in Philadelphia. . . . Time, the great healer. . . .

❖   ❖   ❖   ❖   ❖

The first ordination of American-trained rabbis was . . . an epochal event. . . . Wise and his followers were in a glow of excitement. . . .

Most of the leading rabbis of the country were present. Prominent among them were the examiners, Dr. Kaufmann Kohler of New York, the Reformer; and Rabbis George Jacobs of Philadelphia and Benjamin Szold of Baltimore, the Conservatives. The . . . first class . . . was ordained on the eleventh day of July, 1883. The Rev. Dr. Gustav Gottheil, rabbi of the largest Reform congregation in the country, Temple Emanu-El of New York, delivered the address. . . .

. . . Gottheil and Kohler, the leading Reform rabbis in the east, had not always seen eye to eye with Isaac M. Wise; now they joined in acclaim to the founder of the Hebrew Union College. What thousands had believed impossible had been accomplished. . . . The faith and trust of Isaac M. Wise were justified. His life-work reached its apogee when he laid the hand in blessing upon the heads of his four disciples, Israel Aaron, Henry Berkowitz, Joseph Krauskopf, and David Philipson, and declared them to be rabbis in Israel.

It was a strangely thrilling moment when he pressed the kiss of consecration upon their foreheads. The four young men embodied the hopes of thousands of loyal American Jewish souls. They were setting forth upon a great adventure in the spiritual world. . . .

I have lived through many great moments, but never have I seen a company so exaltingly excited. . . . Men wept for joy and women threw their arms around the necks of the participants. . . .

* * * * *

. . . Dr. Wise asked me to come to his office. . . . I had scarcely entered the room when . . . he said, "You are going to Baltimore." I was startled. . . . He had received a letter from the Har Sinai Congregation asking for one of his graduates. . . . As I was the only graduate who was unplaced in a pulpit it was a Hobson's choice [a choice in which one must take what is offered or nothing].

"But," said I to him, "Doctor, you know that I do not want to take a position this year. I have refused four positions. . . ."

"Ah!" replied he. "But this is different. This is the first offer from an eastern congregation. And, besides, it is the Einhorn congregation. [David Einhorn (1809–1879) was the leader of the extreme wing of the Reform movement and was prominent in anti-slavery movements]. It is a great triumph for us. . . ."

He was really exultant. In vain I pleaded that I would rather teach. . . . I had to set to work at once to write several so-called trial sermons and, horror of horrors, one of them in German! . . . Here was I, an American youth, daring to preach in German to a congregation nurtured on German sermons and a German ritual. . . . My good mother, a cultivated German lady, had always written me letters in German and had insisted that I answer in the same language. But I had never written a German essay or sermon. How I did labor and perspire on that trial German sermon! . . .

I was very graciously received. . . . In the afternoon, a committee . . . offered me the pulpit for three years at a sliding scale of $1,500 the first year, $2,000 the second, and $2,400 the third. . . . Dr. Wise . . . was very happy; he felt that a dent had been made in the eastern opposition, but he advised me not to accept less than $2,000 per annum. I followed his advice and . . . was elected for a term of three years at that figure.

Shortly after I arrived in Baltimore, I matriculated at the Johns Hopkins University as a postgraduate student. One of my classmates in the Semitics department was Cyrus Adler who later became one of the leading figures in American Jewish life. Our friendship continued during more than half a century. . . . Though far apart in our religious interpretation of Judaism, we saw eye to eye in our American outlook.

❀   ❀   ❀   ❀   ❀

. . . I had the feeling that, as a rabbi, it was far more appropriate to have a postgraduate degree from a theological institution. . . . While attending Johns Hopkins I continued my studies at home, looking toward a doctorate from the Hebrew Union College. The requirements . . . were an examination in Bible, *Talmud,* a medieval philosopher, and the submission of a thesis. . . .

. . . I was living in a city that had two unusual libraries, the library of the Johns Hopkins University and of the Peabody Institution. . . . One day, I was struck by the wealth of works on church councils and papal bulls. In a flash the subject for a thesis occurred to me, viz., the relation of the church to the Jews . . . "Church Decrees concerning the Jews from the Third to the Thirteenth Century."

The story that unfolded itself . . . was not a happy one: persecution, repression, and prejudice. I became convinced . . . that the prime cause of anti-Jewish feeling in the Western world is religion, the blaming of Jews for the rejection of Christ. Time and again Judaism was flayed for *caecitas et superstitio,* "blindness and superstition." The Catholic Church was as much opposed to intermarriage as the synagogue. . . . The faithful were forbidden to associate with Jews, to eat with them, to have Jewish physicians treat them, and so on. . . .

When the thesis was finished I sent it to Cincinnati and, upon being informed that it was accepted, I went to Cincinnati, in June, 1886, and took the examination. The faculty . . . conferred the degree of Doctor of Divinity upon me; I was the first graduate of the institution to receive that degree. . . .

✿ ✿ ✿ ✿ ✿

My first direct contact with my rabbinical colleagues in the east . . . took place in January, 1885. I had received a note from Dr. Gustav Gottheil . . . that plans were afoot to form an organization of the rabbis in the eastern states and cordially inviting me to attend. . . .

An organization . . . was effected, with the Rev. Dr. Gustav Gottheil as president and myself as secretary. It adopted the name, Jewish Ministers Association. . . .

. . . Gottheil was a suave diplomat of the pulpit. His was a hand of iron in a velvet glove. The congregation (Temple Emanu-El) was considered the Jewish "cathedral." . . . Most of the prominent Jewish laymen of the city were members. Its beautiful temple of so-called Moorish architecture impressed me greatly. . . .

The other great Reform congregation in New York was Temple Beth-El, of which Dr. Kaufmann Kohler was the rabbi. Kohler was undoubtedly the most scholarly among the New York rabbis. . . . He was of a fiery temperament . . . gloried in controversy and was a fighting champion of the Reform movement. He was a son-in-law of the famous Reformer, Dr. David Einhorn, and [was] his successor in the pulpit of Temple Beth-El.

In Baltimore, I found a religious atmosphere quite different from that in Cincinnati. . . . Isaac M. Wise was the dominant personality in Cincinnati, David Einhorn in Baltimore. True, Einhorn had left Baltimore many years before, but his influence was still potent. During his lifetime, he and Wise had clashed frequently. Einhorn had for his motto, *principiis obsta*, "fealty to principle." Wise had the more statesmanlike outlook. Einhorn was never willing to compromise; Wise felt that life frequently demanded such compromise. Einhorn went forward in a straight line; Wise believed that deviations . . . were often necessary to achieve needed and desirable results.

. . . I had not been in Baltimore long ere an elderly member of the congregation . . . offered to sell me his file of *Sinai*, the magazine edited by Einhorn. . . . This magazine opened an entirely new field. I studied intently the writings of Einhorn.

. . . Thus the two tendencies in the Reform movement found lodgment in my thinking.

THE PRESS Covers the First Sermon of New York's Chief Rabbi, 1888

About 120,000 Jewish families, most of them East European immigrants, lived on the Lower East Side of New York in the 1880s. With only three or four Orthodox rabbis among them, the city's 130 small Orthodox congregations were leaderless, disorganized, and poor. Jewish education, *kashrut,* and religious rituals—marriage, circumcision, burial—were chaotic. Radicals, socialists, and anarchists were pulling the young people away from Judaism, scoffing at Orthodox practices.

The Orthodox community began to organize. The prestigious Congregation Beth Hamidrash Hagadol urged a chief rabbi for New York as there was in England. They began to search in Russia for a suitable rabbi. European rabbis were not eager to immigrate to America. However, Rabbi Jacob Joseph, a leading figure in Vilna, a great spiritual center, finally accepted.

Various segments of the community opposed his election. America was not England, some said, and had no place for a chief rabbi. Reform Jewry feared an immigrant would try to restore "Old Country" ways. Some thought the money should be spent to train American rabbis. Other rabbis envied the salary, the prestige, and publicity of a chief rabbi. The "uptown Jews" looked askance at the rise of the "upstarts" whom they had patronized. And, of course, the radicals had a field day denouncing the venture.

Rabbi Joseph's first sermon was well received, but the honeymoon was short-lived. Problems soon arose regarding ritual and financing. When minimum taxes were levied, a general outcry arose. Wild rumors spread about the chief rabbi's income and alleged profiteering by the Association of American Orthodox

Rabbi Jacob Joseph, New York's chief rabbi, c. 1888. (American Jewish Archives)

Hebrew Congregations. The association began to decline and Rabbi Joseph became a target of attack.

Financially distressed and neglected, the rabbi became ill. On July 28, 1902, fourteen years after his arrival, he died. A praiseworthy effort had ended in a tragic failure.

". . . The glowing faces of the men listening in rapt attention. . . ."

CHIEF RABBI JACOB JOSEPH, the learned Orthodox instructor who was brought to New York from Vilna, Poland, to expound the Mosaic laws for the Orthodox Jews of the East Side, made his first formal appearance yesterday at the synagogue of Beth Hamidrash Hagadol at 54 Norfolk Street. . . .

Ever since Rabbi Joseph's arrival, the Orthodox of his race have been full of excitement and interest. From dawn until late at night they have gathered about his house at 179 Henry Street. . . . The rabbi's doorbell has been going constantly, and several leaders of the congregation have been continually in his house to prevent his being overrun. . . .

The announcement that he would appear in public yesterday threw the eager Hebrews into still greater commotion. The rabbi had . . . said he would deliver a lecture . . . at 4 o'clock in the afternoon.

The trustees of the synagogue . . . made certain that everything was in proper condition. The scrolls containing the Law were safe within the Ark and the light over the Ark, which is never allowed to go out, was burning brightly. It had been arranged not to admit any person not entitled to a seat . . . as the synagogue is not large. . . .

But . . . a crowd entirely filled the street. As far down as Grand Street the sidewalk was packed so that it was next to impossible to force one's way through. . . . President Johns [sic] of the Congregation Beth Hamidrash Hagadol . . . and several others tried to induce the men to fall back and make a clear passageway. Those in the rear were pushing forward, however, and the committee saw that some more serious measure would have to be adopted.

Word was sent to Police Captain Webb and he sent back six policemen. They charged the crowd and plied their clubs but they were only six against a multitude. . . .

Four more policemen were hurried over. The Eldridge Street and Market Street stations also . . . contributed their reserves. Altogether thirty-four policemen were gathered in front of the synagogue. Even then it was with difficulty that the crowd was dispersed. A number of heads were cracked and bruises were plentifully distributed.

Rabbi Joseph had remained entirely unaware of the commotion. A committee of leading Hebrews arrived at his house and found him ready. It being Saturday, riding was out of the question, and he accordingly walked to the synagogue with the committee. He had on his high, soft, black, silk hat made of the shape worn by the High Priest Aaron. A long, black robe fell to his feet. The scattered remnants of the crowd . . . gathered around him and impeded his progress. Had they not been prevented, they would have kissed the hem of his robe. They surrounded him and walked along with him.

Rabbi Joseph is of medium stature and has a coal-black beard which he wears long and divided in the middle. His eyes are black and piercing. . . . The police, under Capt. Webb, escorted the rabbi safely into the synagogue.

. . . When he began to speak, everybody pushed forward, and, while in the front part of the house men were packed like sardines, all the rear rows were empty. In the gallery a number of men sat like Turks in front of the railing while others leaned over them. It made a remarkable picture from below—the glowing faces of the men listening in rapt attention to words from the dark strange figure at the altar. . . .

The services began with prayer by the reader. Then Rabbi Joseph, throwing over his shoulders a wide, white scarf with black stripes at the end, known as a *talis*, ascended the platform.

He spoke slowly . . . frequently pausing to find a word. His quotations were in classical Hebrew, but his general discourse was in a jargon of mixed Polish, German, and Hebrew (Yiddish). . . .

The sermon was not a war cry against the infidels but a reasoned plea for loving kindness and understanding among his adherents.

Rabbi Joseph spoke for just an hour. . . . The services closed with the reading of the scrolls and prayer. Rabbi Joseph held a reception for a short time after that (*Shalosh Seudot*). He was escorted back to his home by Capt. Webb and a force of policemen.

From the *New York Sun*, July 22, 1888

A SCULPTOR Pays Tribute
to His Native East Side, 1880–1902

Should you visit London and walk through the Strand and the British Medical Association Building, you would be awestruck at seeing eighteen giant-sized nude statues. At Hyde Park you could gape at the primitive figures of *Day* and *Night;* you could also view the elemental, almost brutal-looking marbles *Genesis* and *Adam* (the latter weighing three tons).

These are a few of the creations of Sir Jacob Epstein. His sculptures, embracing biblical and diverse themes, are found in some of the world's leading museums. His works include busts of Albert Einstein, Paul Robeson, Chaim Weizmann, Stephen S. Wise, British authors, lords, and commoners.

Born on New York's East Side, in 1880, into a moderately well-to-do family, Epstein studied art at the Educational Alliance Art School and in Paris. In 1905, he settled permanently in London. A prodigious, highly individualistic artist, he had begun his rise to fame by 1907, confident in his integrity as an artist.

For nearly three decades, bitter controversies centered about his works, many of which were described as coarse and repellent. His statues of Christ were considered sacrilegious. But Epstein held his ground, and, when he died in 1959, he was acclaimed the outstanding sculptor of his generation.

"Rembrandt would have delighted in the East Side. . . ."

I CANNOT RECALL a period when I did not draw. Literature and history interested me immensely, and whatever was graphic attracted my attention. Later, I went to the Art Students' League uptown and drew from models and painted a little, but my main studies remained in this quarter where I was born and brought up. When my parents moved to a more respectable and duller part of the city, it held no interest whatever for me. I hired a room in Hester Street in a wooden, ramshackle building that seemed to date back at least a hundred years and, from my window overlooking the market, made drawings daily. I could look down upon the moving mass below and watch them making purchases, bartering, and gossiping. Opposite stood carpenters, washerwomen, and day workers, gathered with their tools in readiness to be hired. Every type could be found here, and for the purpose of drawing I would follow a character until his appearance was sufficiently impressed on my mind for me to make a drawing. A character who interested me particularly was a tall, lean, bearded young man, with the ascetic face of a religious fanatic, who wandered through the streets lost in a profound melancholy. His hair grew to his shoulders, and upon this was perched an old bowler hat. He carried a box in one hand, and, as he passed the pushcarts, the vendors would put food into his box, here an apple, there a herring. He was a holy man, and I followed him into synagogues where he brooded and spent his nights and days.

On one occasion I was taken to see the chief rabbi [see selection 5], a man of great piety who had been brought from Poland to act as the chief rabbi. This sage and holy man lived exactly as he would in a Polish city, with young disciples, in ringlets (*payes*), who attended him as he was very infirm, lifting him into his chair and out of it, and solicitous of his every movement.

The patriarchal simplicity of this house much impressed me. The New York ghetto at that time was a city transplanted from Poland. Parallel with all this was the world of the intelligentsia, the students, journalists, scholars, advanced people, socialists, anarchists, free thinkers, and even "free lovers." Newspapers in Yiddish, Yiddish theaters, literary societies, clubs of all kinds for educational purposes, night classes abounded, and I helped organize an exhibition of paintings and drawings by young men of the quarter. . . .

I kept the room on Hester Street until, on returning to it one morning, I found it burned to the ground and my charred drawings (hundreds of them) floating about in water with dead cats. I had to find another room, this time in a tenement with clothing workers, where I restarted my studies. I never remember giving up this second room; perhaps because of that it has returned to me in dreams with a strange persistence. Even in Paris and in London, in my dreams I find myself in the room as I left it, filled with drawings of the people of the East Side.

The many races in this quarter were prolific. Children by hundreds played upon the hot pavements and in the alleys. Upon the fire escapes and the roofs the tenement dwellers slept for coolness in summer. I knew well the roof life in New York where all East Side boys flew kites; I knew the dock life on the East and West sides; I swam in the East River and the Hudson. To reach the river the boys from the Jewish quarter would have to pass through the Irish quarter; and that meant danger and fights with gangs of that quarter, the children of Irish immigrants.

The Jewish quarter was bounded on one side by the Bowery. At the time, this street was one long line of saloons, crowded at night by visitors to the city, sailors, and prostitutes. As a boy I could watch through the doors at night the strange, garish performers, singers, and dancers; and the whole, turbulent night life was, to my growing, eager mind, of never-ending interest. I recall Steve Brodie's saloon with its windows filled with photographs of famous boxers and the floor inlaid with silver dollars. For a boy a tour along the Bowery was full of excitement. When you reached Chinatown, crooked Mott Street leading to Pell Street, you could buy a stick of sugar cane for one cent and, chewing it, look into the Chinese shop windows, or even go into the temple, all scarlet and gilding, with gilded images. The Chinamen had a curious way of slipping into their houses, suddenly, as into holes; and I used to wonder at the young men with smooth faces like girls. Chinese children were delightful when you saw them, but no Chinese women were to be seen. Along the west front, on the Hudson side, you saw wagons being loaded with large bunches of bananas and great piles of melons. Bananas would drop off the overloaded wagons; you picked them up and continued until you came to the open-air swimming baths with delightful sea water. I was a great frequenter of these swimming places and went there until they shut down in November for the winter.

I haunted the docks and watched the ships from all over the world being loaded and unloaded. Sailors were aloft in the rigging, and along the docks horses and mules drew heavy drays; oyster boats were bringing their loads of oysters and clams; and the shrieks and yells of sirens and the loud cries of overseers made a terrific din. At the Battery, newly arrived immigrants, their shoulders laden with packs, hurried forward; and it must have been with much misgiving that they found their first steps in the New World greeted with the hoots and jeers of hooligans. I can still see them hurrying to gain the Jewish quarter and finding refuge among friends and relatives. I often traveled the great stretch of Brooklyn Bridge, which I crossed hundreds of times on foot, and watched the wonderful bay with its steamers and ferryboats. The New York of the preskyscraper period was my formation ground. I knew all its streets and the waterside; I made excursions into the suburbs: Harlem, Yonkers, Long Island; Coney Island I knew well, and Rockaway where I bathed in the surf. I explored Staten Island, then not yet built upon, and the Palisades with their wild rocks leading down to the Hudson River.

Early on I saw the plastic quality in colored people and had friends among them and later was to work from colored models

Right: Drawings of the people in the Jewish quarter of New York City, by W.A. Rogers, as they appeared in Harper's Weekly, *April 19, 1890. (American Jewish Archives)*

Below: Hester Street on the Lower East Side. (American Jewish Archives)

and friends, including Paul Robeson whose splendid head I worked from in New York. I tried to draw Chinamen in their quarter, but the Chinese did not like being drawn and would immediately disappear when they spotted me. The Italian Mulberry Street was like Naples, concentrated in one swarming district. Within easy reach of one another, I could see the most diverse life from many lands, and I absorbed material which was invaluable.

At this time I was a tremendous reader, and there were periods when I would go off to Central Park and find a secluded place far away from crowds and noise. There I would give myself up to solitary reading for the day and come back home burned by the sun and filled with ideas from Dostoevski's *Brothers Karamazov*, or Tolstoy's novels. . . .

I began to feel at this period that I could more profoundly express myself and give greater reality to my drawings by studying sculpture. I had been drawing and reading to excess, sometimes in dim light, and my eyes had suffered from the strain, so that sculpture gave me relief, and the actual handling of clay was a pleasure.

Naturally my family did not approve of all that I did, although they saw that I had what might be called a special bent. My turning to sculpture was to them mysterious. Later they could not understand why I did certain things any more than the critics who profess to see in me a dual nature—one of the man of talent, and the other the wayward eccentric or the artist who desires to *épater* [shock]. What chiefly concerned my family was why I did things which could not possibly bring me in any money, and they deplored this mad, foolish streak in me. They put it down to the perversity that made me a lonely boy, going off on my own to the woods with a book, and not turning up to meals, and later making friends with Negroes and anarchists. . . .

Saturday in the synagogue was a place of ennui for me, and the wailing prayers would get on my nerves; my one desire would be to make excuses to get away. The picturesque (prayer) shawls with the strange faces underneath held my attention only for a short while, then the tedium of the interminable services would drown every other emotion. Certainly I had no devotional feelings; and later, with my reading and free-thinking ideas, I dropped all practice of ceremonial forms. . . . I was confirmed at the age of thirteen in the usual manner, but how I ever got through this trying ordeal I cannot now imagine. The Passover holidays always interested me for the picturesque meal cere-monies. I remember my father, who was "somebody" in the syna-gogue, bringing home with him one of the poor men who waited outside to be chosen to share the Passover meal. . . . The earnest-ness and simplicity of the old Polish-Jewish manner of living has much beauty in it, and an artist could make it the theme of very fine works. This life is fast disappearing on contact with Ameri-can habits, and it is a pity that there is no Rembrandt of today to draw his inspiration from it before it is too late.

My parents did not discourage me but could not understand how I could make a living by art. Their idea of an artist was a person who was condemned to starvation. Sculpture became to me an absorbing interest. When I started seriously to work, I felt the inadequacies of the opportunity to study. For one thing, only a night class existed in New York. Also, there was very little antique sculpture to be seen, and modern sculpture hardly ex-isted. I longed to go to Paris, and my opportunity came when I met Hutchins Hapgood, the writer, who was very much inter-ested in the East Side. [Hapgood wrote the classic *The Spirit of the Ghetto* which Epstein illustrated.] He asked me to illustrate a book which he had written about it. I drew for him the poets, scholars, actors, and playwrights and also made some drawings of the people. . . .

I was known in the market, and wherever I took up a position to draw I was looked upon sympathetically, and I had no diffi-culty in finding models. Jewish people look upon the work of an artist as something miraculous and love watching him even though they may be extremely critical. I sometimes think I should have remained in New York, the material was so abundant. Wherever one looked there was something interesting—a novel composition, wonderful effects of lighting at night, and picturesque and handsome people. Rembrandt would have delighted in the East Side, and I am surprised that nothing has come out of it, for there is material in New York far beyond anything that American painters hunt for abroad.

From *Let There Be Sculpture*,
by Jacob Epstein,
G.P. Putnam's Sons, 1940, pp. 4–11

MORRIS HILLQUIT Recounts
the Birth of the
Jewish Labor Unions, 1888

The Russian Jews continued to pour in, and this country continued to welcome them. By 1890 the number of Jewish immigrants seeking refuge here reached half a million. In New York City they formed the largest Jewish settlement in the world—as well as the poorest and most congested.

Their helplessness and their needs were so cruelly exploited by employers that it was inevitable that a movement should arise to protect them. Help came from the Socialists who took the initiative in organizing Jewish labor unions—for, at the outset, labor groups were formed on ethnic lines. It was not easy to make an organized force out of these weak, ignorant, and spiritless people, and it was twenty years before the unions were established on a sound basis.

The time came when the United Hebrew Trades merged with other labor groups to form the major labor organizations and the workers they led grew from a mass of timid, submissive individuals into a body of confident, self-respecting men and women.

Latvian-born Morris Hillquit (1870–1933) was one of the youths who helped start the United Hebrew Trades. He later won renown as a lawyer, a spokesman for the worker, and a pacifist. He was the Socialist candidate for mayor of New York twice and for Congress five times; although never elected, he was greatly respected by his fellow citizens.

The problems of getting the labor unions started are described in the following excerpt from Hillquit's autobiography.

*"Penniless and helpless, they were
at the mercy of their employers."*

. . . OUR FAVORITE gathering places were the East Side tea
shops . . . talking and sipping weak tea served in tumblers, Russian style. A glass of tea and a "coffee twist" were, as a rule, the
limit of a guest's consumption. The price of each was five cents. . . .

Of discussion there was plenty, but . . . the enthusiastic young
Socialists . . . cast about for a promising field of practical work
and discovered it among their own countrymen.

In two thousand years of homeless wandering . . . and persecution, the Jewish people had been largely excluded from pro-
ductive work and had become a race of traders and money
lenders. In the New World they evolved for the first time a solid
proletarian bloc.

Many of them turned to the lowest form of trade—peddling;
but that occupation proved utterly inadequate when their numbers rose to hundreds of thousands. . . . The great majority found
work in the clothing industry. Their conditions of life and labor
were pitiful. Penniless and helpless, they were at the mercy of
their employers.

There were hundreds of middlemen in the clothing industry,
in fierce competition with one another. A number of hired sewing machines set up in a tenement-house room, often connected
with their own living quarters, constituted their . . . establishment. In these dark, ill-ventilated, and unsanitary shops a welter
of working and perspiring humanity, men and women . . . were
crowded together. Their pay was nominal, their work hours un-
limited. As a rule they were employed "by the piece," and, as
their work was seasonal and irregular, they were spurred to inhuman exertions. . . .

. . . They were weak from overwork and malnutrition, tired
and listless, meek and submissive. Tuberculosis, the dread plague
of the tenements, was rife among them.

Below: Pushcart peddler. Right: "I Cash Clothes." Above: Sweatshop, Lower East Side. (American Jewish Archives)

. . . We resolved to better the lives of our laboring country-men. . . .

It was a task beset with baffling difficulties. . . . They had not been trained in any form of collective action. They were dull, apathetic, and unintelligent. And, worst of all, we did not speak their language, both figuratively and literally. Our language was Russian. The workers spoke Yiddish. . . .

We all began perfecting our Yiddish. . . .

Taking the bull by the horns, we founded the United Hebrew Trades in October 1888. It was a central labor body without affiliated labor unions, a mere shell. . . .

The organization meeting took place at 25 East Fourth Street, headquarters of the Socialist Labor party. . . .

The only Jewish unions were the Hebrew Typographical Union and the Union of Chorus Singers . . . composed of members of the chorus of the two Yiddish theaters in New York. In the daytime they were employed at other trades. . . . The work at rehearsals and in the nightly performances was strenuous, and the pay [was] three to four dollars a week. But . . . what drove them to seek protection was the brutal treatment . . . by the theater managers.

In membership the two "unions" together represented a grand total of forty. . . .

A somewhat humorous sample of the work ahead of us presented itself at the very first meeting. . . . A delegation from an actors' union applied for affiliation.

The Jewish theaters were in their infancy and had a hard struggle. The members of the troupes were not paid fixed salaries but worked on shares. The lion's share of these "shares" however went to the numerous stars. . . . The class struggle in this instance was between the minor parts and the headliners, and the former formed a union against the latter. . . . We were asked to send a speaker.

The spokesman for the theatrical proletariat was careful to attach proper conditions to his request. Actors are artists, after all, he explained, and cannot be expected to receive instruction in coarse and common Yiddish. Our speaker would have to address them in German, the language of poets and thinkers. All eyes turned on me. I nodded assent. . . . "To have the attention and respect of the audience," he calmly proceeded, "the speaker will have to appear in proper attire, i.e., dressed in frock coat and silk hat."

Again, all eyes turned on me, but this time . . . with consternation succeeded by irrepressible mirth. I was nineteen and looked younger. Frock coats and silk hats were not customary articles of my wardrobe. . . .

. . . The organization meeting of the actors' union was held without our representative and seems to have gotten along quite well, for the Jewish Actors' Union was firmly organized and has remained in . . . existence ever since.

The problem was infinitely more difficult in . . . the needle industry. . . . I remember most vividly the origin of the Knee Pants Makers' Union. . . .

In 1890, there were about 1,000 knee pants makers employed in New York, all "green" (immigrant) and most of them illiterate. It was a sweatshop industry *par excellence*. A contractor employed about ten workers and usually operated his shop in his living-room. . . . He did not even furnish the sewing machines. The operator provided his own machine, needles, and thread. The work day was endless, and the average earnings . . . from six to seven dollars per week. Often the contractor would abscond with a week's pay; often the worker would be discharged because he was not fast enough, and often he would be compelled to quit because of maltreatment or intolerable working conditions. . . . Every time . . . he was compelled to put his sewing machine on his back and carry it to his new place of employment. In early 1890, they struck. The movement was spontaneous, without program, leadership, or organization. It was a blind outbreak of revolt and was destined to collapse if left to itself. . . .

The United Hebrew Trades stepped in. . . . Our first step was to hire a meeting hall large enough to accommodate all the strikers. There were about nine hundred, and . . . we held them in practically continuous session, day and night, allowing them only time to go home to sleep . . . , lest they be tempted to return to work. . . .

While the continuous performance was going on in the main hall, we tried to bring order and system into the strike and to organize the strikers into a solid and permanent union.

We worked out a list of demands centering upon the employer's obligation to furnish sewing machines and other work tools. . . . Then we chose pickets, relief committees, and settlement committees. . . .

The men did not know how to conduct meetings or transact business of any kind. They had never acted in concert. Our discourses on the principles of trade unionism and socialism were interspersed with elementary lessons in parliamentary procedure and practical methods of organization. . . . After one week the contractors weakened; one Saturday night they became panicky and stormed the meeting hall in a body, demanding an immediate and collective settlement on the workers' terms.

The United Hebrew Trades had scored a great victory. . . .

One of the most difficult tasks . . . was the organization of the Jewish bakery workers. . . . Bakeshops had sprung up . . . in deep and dark subcellars, without ventilation or hygienic accommodations. . . . The shops were infested with rats and reeked with dirt. The ovens were primitive. . . .

The new industry employed a few hundred workers, mostly immigrants from Galicia, Hungary, and Poland . . . stolid, unemotional, and irresponsive. They worked seventeen hours to eighteen hours a day, except on Thursday when their "work day" began early in the morning and lasted until noon on Friday. As a rule they boarded and lodged with their employers. They worked at the ovens naked from the waist up and slept in the bakery cellars. . . . When they did not receive board and lodging, their wages averaged six to seven dollars a week. Their only leisure time was between making the dough and its rising, and these hours they spent in their favorite saloons, drinking beer and playing cards.

The beer saloons provided the only romance in their drab lives. Here were their social clubs and their labor bureaus. Here they would exchange information about jobs and here also employers would come in quest of "hands."

Pale-faced, hollow-chested, listless, and brutified, they seemed to be hopeless material for organization and struggle.

Anxious to remove them from the demoralizing atmosphere of the Ludlow Street saloon, the national organization of bakery workers had secured new headquarters for them . . . back of a beer saloon on Orchard Street. Meeting halls connected with saloons were customary for labor unions in those days. The saloon keeper would make no charge for the room, expecting to be compensated in trade. In the case of the German and Irish unions the scheme worked well, but with the Jewish unions it mostly proved unprofitable. . . .

The attempted removal of the Jewish bakers from the Ludlow Street saloon met with considerable opposition. They were used to their old gathering place. . . . To the Jewish bakery workers the class struggle assumed the form of a fight between two rival saloons. . . . The anti-union Ludlow Street saloon won out. The union disbanded.

. . . The United Hebrew Trades launched a new campaign to organize the bakers in 1889. . . .

The principal demand was for the six-day week with one day of rest, on Saturdays, a radical demand in those days.

The strike call met with general response. The Jewish bakeshops were tied up and, within a few days, surrendered. . . .

A tragic incident . . . served to call public attention to the revolting conditions in bakeshops. . . .

One early morning the secretary reported to the United Hebrew Trades that a baker had collapsed while working at night and was still in the bakeshop, critically ill. . . . When Weinstein reached the bakery cellar, he found a most appalling condition of filth, with three emaciated and exhausted bakers continuing to work at the side of their agonizing comrade. He arranged to have the sick man taken to a hospital and reported the case to the Labor Department. . . .

An investigation of the bakeshops . . . resulted in a sensational report, condemning their inhuman labor conditions and branding them as a menace to public health.

. . . The New York State legislature enacted a law, limiting work in bakeries to ten hours a day. . . . The employers fought it in all courts of the state. . . . In the United States Supreme Court it was reversed by a vote of five to four.

"There is no reasonable ground for interfering with the liberty of person or the right of free contract, by determining the hours of labor, in the occupation of a baker," declared Mr. Justice Peckham. . . . "There is no contention that bakers, as a class, are not equal in intelligence and capacity to men in other trades . . . or that they are not able to assert their rights . . . without the protecting arm of the state interfering with their independence of judgment and of action."

The learned court held that the law curtailed both "the right of the individual to labor for such time as he may choose" and the right of the employer "to purchase labor" . . . as he may choose.

I have often wondered whether Mr. Justice Peckham and his four concurring associates would have felt quite so certain about the capacity of the bakers to assert their rights . . . if they had . . . seen the sovereign and independent baker who fell in the midst of this free labor like an overburdened beast. And I am still wondering why a few theorists, ignorant of the daily struggles and sufferings of the toiling masses, should be allowed to determine industrial relations, social conflicts, and human rights. . . .

. . . With the immediate object of their strike attained, the members lost interest in their organization and . . . disbanded. The lack of organization led to a new deterioration of labor standards and to a new revolt, another strike, and a revival of the union, followed by an inevitable decline. . . . The disheartening process was repeated . . . every two or three years . . . until stability and permanence were at last achieved.

Such was the history of . . . practically all other Jewish trade unions. . . .

In the minds of Jewish workers of that period, unions were little more than instruments of strikes. They were mostly born in strikes and died with the end of the strikes. . . . It was not until about 1910 that the Jewish labor movement was organized on a solid and stable basis.

From *Loose Leaves from a Busy Life,*
by Morris Hillquit, The MacMillan Co.,
1934, pp. 15-28

A JEWISH ANARCHIST Reminisces about the Yom Kippur Balls, 1889

In the din and clamor of the ghetto there was one shortlived radical movement, Jewish anarchism, that declared war against God and did everything conceivable to deride Judaism and all its observances. To its adherents, all religions were allies of the state and capitalism which they resolved to extirpate. They published a weekly called *Freie Arbeiter Shtime* (*Free Workers' Voice*), which had a circulation of 3,500, and several other publications, all calculated to subvert the Jewish faith, ritual, and observance.

To dramatize their campaign, the anarchists concentrated their assault on *Yom Kippur,* the holiest day of the Jewish year. On *Kol Nidre* night they arranged dances. They organized parades with taunting banners; while marching they ate *trefah* (forbidden) foods and derided the Day of Atonement. They printed and distributed derisive parodies of the *Yom Kippur* liturgy.

Ultimately their war against God became self-destructive. While many individuals persisted in espousing the anarchist ideology, anarchism as a group manifestation was rooted out of Jewish life.

". . . If there is a God let Him fight His own battles."

IN THE YEAR 1889, the anarchists in America strained their resources and issued an organ in Yiddish, *Di Varheit* (The Truth), in which, of course, they devoted considerable space to propaganda against religion. They went even farther; five months later, when *Di Varheit* failed . . . just before the High Holy Days, they circulated a propaganda sheet which they named *Tefilah Zakah* [the *Yom Kippur* prayer of purity].

These *Tefilah Zakah* parodies, aside from being powerful propaganda media, were well written. They produced an even greater effect than the publishers had expected. The first *Tefilah Zakah* was published in 1889. It treated the theme that, from the time of Revelation on Mount Sinai until after the Babylonian Exile, the Jews did not observe the Day of Atonement. This created a tremendous furor!

The second *Tefilah Zakah* parodied the prayer *Ki Hineh Kachomer* [the prayer which begins, "For like clay are we in the potter's hands"] as well as other . . . prayers in the High Holy Day prayer book. It, too, found favor with the public.

The *Tefilah Zakah* parodies were issued regularly in thousands of copies. . . . They shocked the Jewish public and left a profound effect. . . .

Another temerarious means which the Pioneers [anarchists] employed in their struggle against religion was the *Yom Kippur* ball.

It happened in the year 1889. The Pioneers had rented the Clarendon Hall on Thirteenth Street for *Yom Kippur* eve, the night of *Kol Nidre* [the well-known prayer chanted on the eve of the Day of Atonement]. The Pioneers gave out thousands of leaflets . . . in shops and factories on the East Side. Some bolder Jewish *shkotzim* [ruffians] gave them out even near the synagogues. The leaflets called the Jewish workers to come and enjoy a pleasant evening at a ball instead of going to the synagogues to ask forgiveness for sins and transgressions which not they but their "bosses" had committed.

The announcement of the *Yom Kippur* ball fell like a bombshell in the Jewish quarter. The Orthodox element[s] were terribly upset. The very attempt at such a deed angered them deeply. This could not be possible! It just couldn't be true! It couldn't happen. They called meetings; they called on their Ger-

man brethren to aid them; they turned to the Jewish politicians
. . . to help prevent such sacrilege. Finally they found a "savior,"
one Levy, coroner of the state of New York. He made contact
with powerful politicians who persuaded the police to influence
the owner of the hall (a saloon keeper who depended upon police
favors) to break his contract with the Pioneers and prevent the
ball from taking place. The police . . . exerted pressure upon
the proprietor, promised him the moon and the stars, and pledged
their word that in return for this "favor" he would be rewarded.
They also took it upon themselves to cover damage costs which
the owner might incur.

It is almost impossible for me to describe the scene that took
place around Clarendon Hall that *Yom Kippur* eve.

Thousands upon thousands of people crowded the streets . . . ;
many workers came with their wives and children, not knowing
that the ball was canceled. Many curious people left their synagogues and came to see what would happen. In addition . . .
many religious hoodlums came to fight the Lord's battle with
sticks in their hands.

The owner refused to open the hall. . . . A cry of protest arose
which echoed in the streets. Our opponents were not silent
either. They caused such a tumult that the police . . . began to
scatter the crowds giving the usual excuse that they must clear
the streets.

I was not a member of the Pioneers then, yet I succeeded in
entering the hall. A crowd of reporters . . . encircled me and
showered me with questions. I could not give them precise an-
swers. . . .

. . . Nevertheless, the entire press came out the next morning
with whole pages filled with fictitious reports in the minutest
details about the extraordinary event, thereby rendering the
Pioneers and their antireligious propaganda publicity which they
did not think possible.

The anarchist crowd and the sympathizers gathered that night
in the "locale" of the Pioneers which was situated (irony of
ironies!) in a city-owned building and composed strong, moving

protests. Through the night they printed these flyers and early the next morning, when the worshippers went to *shul* [synagogue], distributed them in the thousands. I, and Hilkowitch . . . who is now a lawyer, sweated over . . . this statement. The headline of the leaflet bore in large letters: "The finger of God— a policeman's club!" The text expressed the idea: "If there is a God let Him fight His own battles." It ridiculed the Orthodox who like dumb oxen were frightened to death of a red flag. Instead of appealing to God and waiting for His help, these religious fanatics appealed to the police who came to their immediate assistance.

Financially the Pioneers became rich from the canceled ball. The owner of the hall, fearing reprisal from labor organizations . . . appeased the Pioneers with . . . five hundred dollars—an outstandingly large sum for those times—and . . . because of the disrupted ball the Pioneers had gained more . . . than if it had taken place.

The complete episode, the audacity and courage of the Pioneers, formed a very strong impression on those radicals who until this point kept their distance. . . . Now, many of them came closer to the Jewish anarchistic group in which they enrolled as members. I was one of them.

Translated from the Yiddish by the editor

From *Amol in America* (*Long Ago in America*),
by Israel Kopelioff, Charles Brzoza,
Warsaw, 1928, pp. 234-39

LILLIAN D. WALD Changes American City Life, 1893

For young Lillian Wald it took only half an hour, visiting with a sick woman in a wretched, overcrowded two-room, rear "apartment," to change her entire life and the life of the American city. "A baptism of fire," she called that visit. From then on, she became a beacon, a standard bearer for the forces of social progress.

It is in large measure because of her vision, example, utter dedication, and fighting spirit that today we have the Visiting Nurse Service; low income public housing; neighborhood institutions such as nursery schools, music schools, theater groups, mental hygiene clinics, summer camps for underprivileged children, and workshops for the elderly; and medicare. These social improvements were initiated by Miss Wald from her modest headquarters, known as the Henry Street Settlement on the Lower East Side, which became her home and laboratory in 1893.

Lillian Wald championed the causes of her neighbors whose problems she knew first hand. She arbitrated strikes and implacably stood up against corrupt politicians. Reared in a German Jewish well-to-do family, she was able to interpret the plight of the Eastern European Jews to the affluent uptown German Jews and to enlist their cooperation to improve the lot of the poor immigrants. Her successful house on Henry Street became a prototype for similar projects in other large city slums.

". . . But five of the seven children are nearly naked."

VISIT and care of typhoid patient, 182 Ludlow Street. Visit to 7 Hester Street where in rooms of Nathan S. found two children with measles. After much argument succeeded in bathing these two patients and the sick baby. The first time in their experience. They insisted no water and soap could be applied to anyone with measles before seven days. Brought clean dresses to the older children.

. . . Spoke to the father about moving family away from the wretched house, advising country is less crowded. . . . He explained that being near people who could understand their language was sole influence on their choice of residence, professing to despise the filth and vermin. Upon his promising to seek employment elsewhere, I agreed that, if he moved to the country, we would give the children shoes and assist in their respectable appearance in their new home.

Gave tickets for Hebrew Sanitarium excursion to Mrs. D. and three children, Mrs. S. and five children.

. . . But five of the seven children are nearly naked. I am convinced they have no apparel . . . so we will make their decent appearance possible for the picnic. Visited both families and rooms, and an effort is really being made to keep them and the children cleaner. . . .

At luncheon Miss Loeb (one of the visiting nurses) reports Mrs. L., 11 Rutgers Street, basement, consented to go to German hospital. Horrible tales of a child's immorality, her presence being a menace to the children of both sexes of the tenement. With the mother's consent, I reported her to the Gerry Society [a New York organization, founded in 1865, for the prevention of cruelty to children]. . . .

Case of Mrs. G., 183 Clinton Street, rear tenement, second floor. First found by Miss Brewster, July 1st, *puerperal septicemia* [a form of blood poisoning], lying on vermin-infested bed without sheets or pillow cases. Husband, a peddler, had $40 saved

An East Side tenement which often doubled as a sweatshop. (American Jewish Archives)

at beginning of illness, three weeks before. All had gone and none coming in, for he had been obliged to remain home to care for five children and wife. Dr. T. in attendance had been receiving 75 cents a visit. . . . Woman's place was cleaned, beef and wine obtained from United Hebrew Charities. Carefully nursed, and husband, after much argument upon the economy of it, agreed to pay a woman $3 a week to wash the clothes, look after the children all day, while he resumed his work. After much labor a Jewish woman was obtained for such service but impossible for less than $6 per week. We are paying the other $3. The husband is capable of making $4 a day, so they will soon be on their feet. . . . We started the children in Penny Provident Bank of the College Settlement. Despite their exceeding poverty, the children are being taught the thrift of penny saving.

Mrs. E., 3 Sheriff Street. Her leg has been treated by Miss B. It merely needed clean bandaging. She did scrub her rooms once but, as both husband and wife drink and they are old, Miss B. thinks time wasted to attempt reformation. Will confine herself to physical help.

Case of Hannah R., 7 Hester Street, rear tenement, first floor. Upon repeated investigation found the woman suffering from a bad hernia, and washing or earning her living of course impossible by hand labor. I fear she is hopelessly unclean for the children are only washed and the rooms cleansed when she sees me approach. The truss was needed, and yesterday she wore it for the first time. The Forty-second Street dispensary fitted her gratis at request of United Hebrew Charities.

Opposite a Russian family, name of H. The father has obtained work in Newark but leaves family here as they have not saved money to move. Saturday, when the husband is in New York, I will persuade him to move (the wife has already consented) for . . . Mr. Solomon of the Baron de Hirsch Fund has agreed to pay transportation.

Annie P., 44 Allen Street, front tenement, second floor. Husband Louis P. came here three years ago and one year ago sent for wife and three children. From that time, unfortunately, his trade, that of shoemaker, became less remunerative. She helped by washing and like labor, but two months ago he deserted her, though she stoutly maintains that he returned to Odessa to get his old work back. The youngest, Meyer P., age 5, fell from table and injured his hip. He lay for seven months in the Orthopedic Hospital, Forty-second Street; [he] was discharged as incurable and supplied with a brace. The mother is absolutely tied by her pregnant condition; the cripple is in pain and cries to be carried. They had no rooms of their own but paid $3 a month to Hannah A., a decent tailoress, who allowed the family to sleep on her floor. The $3 cannot be forthcoming now for the woman's accouchement [delivery in childbirth] is in three weeks. The children are unusually attractive, and later investigation showed that they all told the exact truth. . . . Monday, I filed application with Montefiore Home for Meyer's admission. The New York Hospital promised to look after the child until place was secured—if not too long. Tuesday, I went to Hebrew Sheltering Guardian Society . . . and obtained promise of place for the two well children by Thursday afternoon. Necessary to procure committal first. Mr. Jenkins of SPCC [Society for the Prevention of Cruelty to Children] made it urgent and obtained Judge Ryan's signature Thursday morning. Thursday afternoon, we washed and dressed the two children, and I left them . . . at the asylum, leaving my address for the superintendent so that he might know their friend in case of need. They have absolutely no one in America but their mother. As soon as an answer is received from Montefiore . . . I will take the mother to the Nursery and Child's Hospital where she will be cared for during confinement.

From "Case Notes of Lillian Wald, July 7, 1893,"
reported in *The New York Times*, January 18, 1895,
as quoted in *Portal to America: The Lower East Side, 1870–1925*,
Allon Schoener, editor, Holt, Rinehart & Winston, 1967

AN ALUMNUS Looks Back on the Early Years at the Baron de Hirsch Jewish Agricultural School in Woodbine, New Jersey, 1894

The "Back to the Soil" movement which arose with such enthusiasm soon began to founder. Jewish farm colonies, which had sprung up all over the United States, were disintegrating. The settlers could not cope with the isolation, the barriers of language and culture, their unpreparedness for agriculture, the lack of equipment, their deep yearnings to live as Jews, and other difficulties. The situation looked dismal. But, in 1894, a new start was made with the establishment of the Baron de Hirsch Jewish Agricultural School in Woodbine, New Jersey.

Heading this effort was Professor Wolf Hirsch Sabsovitch, a founder of the Odessa *Am Olam* group (see selection 3). A practical idealist, he had prepared himself for agronomy in universities of Switzerland and the United States. He rejected an offer to teach agricultural chemistry at Wyoming College and chose instead to lay the foundations of the Jewish Agricultural School in southern New Jersey, the cradle of the Jewish farm movement.

Sabsovitch started with a group of fifteen students who were sons of the Woodbine pioneers. Some years later, Arthur Goldhaft wrote about his studies in the school in his autobiography, *The Golden Egg*. It is a unique document, the first to record the education of an American Jewish agriculturalist during these pioneering days.

"Mama received the biggest ovation of all. . . ."

WHEN I CAME to the school it was quite an impressive establishment. Besides the model dairy, the poultry run with its incubators, utterly newfangled then, there was an apiary, a plant nursery, [and] a weather bureau on a fifty-foot tower. There were blacksmithing shops, there was a carpentry. Even rudimentary veterinary science was taught. But the thing that impressed me most was the sight of a baseball team.

And, I noticed right away, there were also girls. Some fifteen girls, carefully sequestered in a special dormitory among the teachers' cottages, were being given courses in domestic science, as well as in the hothouse and in poultry—the traditional women's chores on the farm.

We woke at six-thirty and took cold showers, a real innovation. After breakfast, we worked for about three hours on the farm whose fields spread over 300 acres. At ten, we had a second breakfast and time for a rest, even a nap. Then our schoolwork started.

We had courses in botany, chemistry, physiology, taught by Prof. Sabsovitch himself. There was Frederick Schmidt to teach us practical farm subjects, poultry raising, which didn't especially interest me at that time, and beekeeping and dairying. I took more to the horses and experienced a great pride the first day I could hitch up a horse to a plough. I have never really lost the sense of excitement of walking barefoot on a ploughed field. . . .

There were also the general educational subjects, history, geography, mathematics, at the school.

We were encouraged in cultural interests, too, for the Sabsovitches had brought with them the love of music and reading . . . we even had drawing lessons.

Nowadays, of course, there are scores of fine state agricultural colleges. But at the time there was no institution that could have done for us what the Baron de Hirsch school did.

For the first time, I felt I was living a life. There were plenty of activities, besides the sports, in which I was soon immersed. We had a band, of course, and debating societies. . . .

We were welcomed in town where there were drama circles, and musicales and lectures.

We even had "strikes." They were more than protests, they were a kind of spiritual action—an assertion of personality. Once when there was no butter in the dining hall due to some mixup in purchasing, the "firebrands" among us immediately called a strike. Jam was substituted, but still we struck. Prof. Sabsovitch . . . took this quite seriously . . . and called a big assembly and told us he was disappointed in us.

It was a good three years, and I was graduating. Something happened at the graduation that [to me] was unforgettable.

Though my father didn't come for the ceremony, my mother made her way out to Woodbine, dressed in her best. The auditorium was filled. In our smart uniforms, with our capes over our shoulders, we felt like West Pointers. Our European classmates were now Americans, too.

I was the salutatorian, second in the class, which made Mama extremely proud since she had always feared for my future as a scholar. There I was on the platform, trying to remember my speech and, particularly, to keep in mind the names of all of the dignitaries I had to welcome. I got through without an omission.

The exercises were just about over, and Prof. Sabsovitch was bidding us a fond farewell, when I was startled to see my mother rising up in one of the back rows. "Honorable Mr. Isaacs," she began, "I would like to say something."

All heads turned to stare in amazement at the tiny woman. And, in that first moment, I wanted to sink through the platform. For my first reaction, I am ashamed to say, was shame. . . . I was afraid this little woman with her Yiddish accent would make a fool of me . . . before all these dignitaries, these important American leaders and millionaires.

But, as she began to talk, it was as . . . when Mama talked to me, to show me what was right in the world. "Please," she was saying, "I want to say what is in my heart, what a wonderful thing you are doing here in this school, for my boy, for these boys. You are doing what we by ourselves can't do for them. To make them into fine people. We came here 'greenhorns,' and we want our children should be different, to have a different way of life, and we can't bring it to them and you are bringing it. So I want to say that we know, that a mother knows how her boy is becoming different, a good Jewish boy and an American, and a man in this world, with something he can do, a way to live, like we tried, but we couldn't do it. We came to try to be like a new people who could do things on the land like anybody else, but we didn't know how. Now the Baron [de Hirsch] understood and made this school here, and the professors, the American professors, too, not only Jewish people, came here for our boys. . . ."

I had stopped feeling afraid. I looked around, and everyone was listening to her with respect. Prof. Sabsovitch was leaning almost out of his seat.

"So I wanted to say what is in my heart, to thank you—" she was saying, "to give thanks, not only for what you did for my boy, but for every boy in the school." And she said, "I am sure, just as sure like I am standing here on the floor talking, that every boy and girl that is graduating will be a different person because of this school, and will be an honest man and a good citizen because of this school, and will remember this school to do good in his life because he saw here there were people that wanted to do him good. So thanks, thanks from the heart." She ended, and I saw, all over the hall, people were applauding. On the platform too! And I saw Mrs. Amram was crying! The applause grew louder, louder than for Prof. Sabsovitch; louder than for the Baron's own representative, Mr. Isaacs; louder than for the millionaire, Mr. Schiff. Mama received the biggest ovation of all. . . .

From *The Golden Egg*, by Arthur Goldhaft, pp. 94–100.
Reprinted by permission of the publisher,
Horizon Press, New York, Copyright 1957

EDNA FERBER Remembers
Her Early Childhood in Iowa, 1895

Edna Ferber (1885–1968) was a celebrated American novelist, playwright, and short-story writer. Among her best sellers dramatized for the stage and screen were *Show Boat, Cimarron, Dinner at Eight* (written with George S. Kaufman), and *Giant.* The autobiography of her early life, *A Peculiar Treasure* (based on Exodus 19:5: "Ye [the Children of Israel] shall be my own treasure"), is an affirmation of her faith.

As a young child she lived for a while in Ottumwa, Iowa, a grimy coal mining town of 16,000, whose population was unlettered, bigoted, and anti-Semitic. Edna found an escape from her sordid surroundings in reading works by Horatio Alger, Mark Twain, Charles Dickens, and George Eliot. Her native talents were quickened by her extensive reading and bore rich fruit early in her career.

". . . These Ottumwa years were more enriching, more valuable than all the fun and luxury of the New York years."

ON SATURDAYS, and on unusually busy days when my father could not take the time to come home to the noon dinner, it became my duty to take his midday meal down to him, very carefully packed in a large basket: soup, meat, vegetables, dessert. This must be carried with the utmost care so as not to spill or slop. No one thought of having a sandwich and a cup of coffee in the middle of the day, with a hot dinner to be eaten at leisure in the peace of the evening.

This little trip from the house on Wapello Street to the store on Main Street amounted to running the gauntlet. I didn't so much mind the Morey girl. She sat in front of her house perched on the white gatepost, waiting, a child about my age, with long red curls, a freckled face, very light green eyes. She swung her long legs idly. At sight of me her listlessness fled.

"Hello, Sheeny!" Then variations on this. This, one learned to receive equably. Besides, the natural retort to her baiting was to shout, airily, "Redhead! Wets the bed!"

But as I approached the Main Street corner there sat a row of vultures perched on the iron railing at the side of Sargent's drugstore. These were not children, they were men. Perhaps to me, a small child, they seemed older than they were, but their ages must have ranged from eighteen to thirty. There they sat, perched on the black iron rail, their heels hooked behind the lower rung. They talked almost not at all. The semicircle of spit rings grew richer and richer on the sidewalk in front of them. Vacant-eyed they stared and spat and sat humped and round-shouldered, doing nothing, thinking nothing, being nothing. Suddenly their lackluster eyes brightened, they shifted, they licked their lips a little and spat with more relish. From afar they had glimpsed their victim, a plump little girl in a clean starched gingham frock, her black curls confined by a ribbon bow.

Every fiber of me shrieked to run the other way. My eyes felt hot and wide. My face became scarlet. I must walk carefully so as not to spill the good hot dinner. Now then. Now.

"Sheeny! Has du gesek de Isaac! De Moses! De Levi! Heh, Sheeny, what you got!" Good Old Testament names. They doubtless heard them in their Sunday worship but did not make the connection, quite. They then brought their hands, palms up, above the level of their shoulders and wagged them back and forth, "Oy-yoy, Sheeny! Run! Go on, run!"

I didn't run. I glared. I walked by with as much elegance and aloofness as was compatible with a necessity to balance a basket of noodle soup, pot roasts, potatoes, vegetables, and pudding.

Of course it was nothing more than a couple of thousand years of bigotry raising its hideous head again to spit on a defenseless and shrinking morsel of humanity. Yet it all must have left a deep scar on a sensitive child. It was unreasoning and widespread in the town. My parents were subject to it. The four or five respectable Jewish families of the town knew it well. They were intelligent men and women, American-born and bred, for the most part. It probably gave me a ghastly inferiority, and out of that inferiority doubtless was born inside me a fierce resolution, absurd and childish, such as, "You wait! I'll show you! I'll be rich and famous and you'll wish you could speak to me."

Well, I did become rich and famous and have lived to see entire nations behaving precisely like the idle, frustrated bums perched on the drugstore railing. Of course, Ottumwa wasn't a benighted town because it was cruel to its Jewish citizens. It was cruel to its Jewish citizens because it was a benighted town. Business was bad, the town was poor, its people were frightened, resentful, and stupid. There was, for a place of its size and locality, an unusually large rough element. As naturally as could be, these searched for a minority on whom to vent their dissatisfaction with the world. And there they were, and there I was, the scapegoat of the ages. Yet, though I had a tough time of it in Ottumwa and a fine time of it in New York, I am certain that these Ottumwa years were more enriching, more valuable than all the fun and luxury of the New York years.

New England awoke, horrified and ashamed, after its orgy of witch burning. Ottumwa must feel some embarrassment at the recollection of its earlier ignorance and brutality. A Nazi-infested world may one day hide its face at the sight of what it has wrought in its inhuman frenzy.

MARY ANTIN Writes an Ode to George Washington, 1896

The most effective early agency of Americanization was the public school. Jewish immigrant children, who had experienced anti-Semitism in the Old World, profoundly appreciated the freedom America offered and radiated their love for their adopted homeland.

Well do I recall how warmly I was received when I enrolled in public school at the age of eleven. I was older than my classmates and had come from a *shtetl* whose background was almost medieval. My English was clumsy; I interchanged the pronunciation of the "V" and the "W." But it did not take long to adjust, to be accepted, and even to rise to the top of the class.

School and home were as one. Jews, who were always imbued with a respect for learning, instilled in their children a desire to study. The children felt themselves expounders of American democracy and taught English to their Yiddish-speaking parents who much appreciated their efforts. This mutual attitude speeded the adjustment process to the new ways of life.

Authoress and social worker Mary Antin (1881–1949) was deeply affected by the dream and reality of America. Brought up in Boston, where she had arrived with her family in 1892, she articulated her feelings in a book, *The Promised Land,* which was a panegyric to her adopted homeland. For many years, chapters of her book were used as text material in Massachusetts public schools.

Below we catch a glimpse of her adoration for the Father of the Republic in a piece which she wrote when she was about eleven years old.

"The name I wished to celebrate was the most difficult of all. Nothing but 'Washington' rhymed with 'Washington'."

On THE DAY of the Washington celebration I recited a poem that I had composed in my enthusiasm. But "composed" is not the word. The process of putting on paper the sentiments that seethed in my soul was really very discomposing. I dug the words out of my heart, squeezed the rhymes out of my brain, forced the missing syllables out of their hiding places in the dictionary. May I never again know such travail of the spirit as I endured during the fevered days when I was engaged on the poem. It was not as if I wanted to say that snow was white or grass was green. I could do that without a dictionary. It was a question now of the loftiest sentiments, of the most abstract truths, the names of which were very new in my vocabulary. It was necessary to use polysyllables, and plenty of them; and where to find rhymes for such words as "tyranny," "freedom," and "justice" when you had less than two years' acquaintance with English! The name I wished to celebrate was the most difficult of all. Nothing but "Washington" rhymed with "Washington." It was a most ambitious undertaking, but my heart could find no rest till it had proclaimed itself to the world; so I wrestled with my difficulties and spared no ink, till inspiration perched on my penpoint, and my soul gave up its best.

When I had done, I was myself impressed with the length, gravity, and nobility of my poem. My father was overcome with emotion as he read it. His hands trembled as he held the paper to the light, and the mist gathered in his eyes. My teacher, Miss Dwight, was plainly astonished at my performance and said many kind things and asked many questions. . . . When Miss Dwight asked me to read my poem to the class on the day of celebration, I readily consented. It was not in me to refuse a chance to tell my schoolmates what I thought of George Washington.

I was not a heroic figure when I stood up in front of the class to pronounce the praises of the Father of his Country. Thin, pale, and hollow, with a shadow of short black curls on my brow . . . I must have looked more frightened than imposing. My dress added no grace to my appearance. . . . Heels clapped together, and hands glued to my sides, I lifted up my voice in praise of George Washington. It was not much of a voice; like my hollow cheeks, it suggested consumption. My pronunciation was faulty, my declamation flat. But I had the courage of my convictions. I was face to face with two score fellow citizens. . . . I must tell what George Washington had done for their country—for me.

I can laugh now at the impossible meters, the grandiose phrases, the verbose repetitions of my poem. Years ago I must have laughed at it when I threw my only copy into the waste-basket. The copy I am now turning over was loaned to me by Miss Dwight who faithfully preserved it all these years for the sake, no doubt, of what I strove to express when I laboriously hitched together those dozen and more ungraceful stanzas. But, to the forty fellow citizens sitting in rows in front of me, it was no laughing matter. Even the bad boys sat in attitudes of attention, hypnotized by the solemnity of my demeanor. . . . I fixed their eighty eyes with my single stare and gave it to them, stanza after stanza, with such emphasis as the lameness of the lines permitted.

> He whose courage, will, amazing bravery
>   Did free his land from a despot's rule,
> From man's greatest evil, almost slavery,
>   But all that's taught in tyranny's school,
> Who gave his land its liberty,
>   Who was he?
>
> 'Twas he who e'er will be our pride,
>   Immortal Washington,
> Who always did in truth confide.
>   We hail our Washington!

The best of the verses were no better than these, but the children listened. They had to. Presently I gave them news, declaring that Washington

Wrote the famous Constitution; sacred's the hand
That this blessed guide to man had given, which says, "One
And all of mankind are alike, excepting none."

This was received in respectful silence, possibly because the other fellow citizens were as hazy about historical facts as I at this point. . . . For I made myself the spokesman of the "luckless sons of Abraham," saying—

Then we weary Hebrew children at last found rest
In the land where reigned Freedom, and like a nest
To homeless birds your land proved to us, and therefore
Will we gratefully sing your praise evermore.

The boys and girls who had never been turned away from any door because of their father's religion sat as if fascinated in their places. But they woke up and applauded heartily when I was done, following the example of Miss Dwight who wore the happy face which meant that one of her pupils had done well.

The recitation was repeated, by request, before several other classes, and the applause was equally prolonged at each repetition. After the exercises, I was surrounded, praised, questioned, and made much of by teachers as well as pupils. Plainly I had not poured my praise of George Washington into deaf ears. The teachers asked me if anybody had helped me with the poem. The girls invariably asked, "Mary Antin, how could you think of all those words?" None of them thought of the dictionary!

If I had been satisfied with my poem in the first place, the applause with which it was received by my teachers and schoolmates convinced me that I had produced a very fine thing indeed. So the person, whoever it was—perhaps my father—who suggested that my tribute to Washington ought to be printed did not find me difficult to persuade. When I had achieved an absolutely perfect copy of my verses, at the expense of a dozen sheets of blue-ruled note paper, I crossed the Mystic River to Boston and boldly invaded Newspaper Row.

From *The Promised Land* (Tauschnitz Edition),
by Mary Antin, 1913, pp. 237-241.
Reprinted by permission of the publisher, Houghton Mifflin Company

ABRAHAM CAHAN Passes Around the Hat to Collect for the Jewish Daily Forward, 1897

In the late 1880s a number of Yiddish labor newspapers were founded, among them the *Arbeiter Zeitung,* the *Varheit,* and *Folks-Zeitung.* "Abe" Cahan, later one of the leaders of the Jewish socialist labor movement, opposed the cliques that dominated these organs. He compared them to the members of the British House of Lords whose office was hereditary. He fought for the election of representatives and the democratization of the movement. (For the story of Abraham Cahan up to the time he became editor of the *Jewish Daily Forward,* read *The Education of Abraham Cahan,* translated from the Yiddish, Jewish Publication Society, 1969.)

On December 30 and 31, 1897, representatives of twenty-three organizations, affiliated with socialist and trade unions—which Cahan called the "House of Commons"—met in the basement of Valhalla Hall in New York. They formed an association to found a socialist daily for Yiddish-speaking working people. The name proposed for the paper was the *Forward,* the name of the party organ of the German Socialists. Abe Cahan was duly elected editor. Funds to launch the paper were obtained through appeals to working people. The *Forvertz* (*Forward*) was founded from the "hat collections" passed around at mass meetings of these Jewish workers.

"People removed rings and wristwatches and threw them into the pile."

I SHALL never forget a mass meeting which we called in order to collect money for the proposed new paper. It was held in the large basement of the Valhalla Hall on Orchard Street. . . . After the appeal we started the collections. I and another (I think it was Winchevsky) [Morris Winchevsky was a prominent Yiddish poet and publicist.] went around, our hats in hand, to collect the contributions. The audience responded generously, some donating ten-dollar, five-dollar, two-dollar bills, and silver coins. People removed rings and wristwatches and threw them into the pile. I recall how heavy my hat became that I had to hold it with both hands it should not rip open.

I remember a few heartwarming incidents. When a man took out his pocketbook to give a dollar, his wife demanded, "Give me also a dollar to throw in." He made a grimace to indicate that one dollar is sufficient. In protest the woman pulled off one ring from her finger, then another, and threw them into the hat.

An old man approached me and whispered, "I have no money with me, but I will send my contribution later. You can trust me. I will not eat or drink; my contribution I shall not fail to send."

These years (1925–28) a five-dollar contribution is not impressive. Then [1890s] it was a big sum. And yet many gave five- and ten-dollar gifts. Some pawned their valuables. I can cite the instance of a certain comrade, who pawned his new suit to participate in giving to the fund.

Max Pine [a labor leader and communal figure, 1866–1928] remembers a similar scene at another fund-raising meeting. An ash pale little fellow, a capmaker, approached the chairman slowly and laid down a $25 bill. "Twenty-five dollars," the chairman cried out in amazement. The little man nods silently. An excited group surrounds him and people begin to throw money into the hat. Some sign their names, pledging that they will contribute later. . . . Others give rings, watches, bracelets, and other valuables. . . .

It was dawn when the meeting ended.

Translated from the Yiddish by the editor

From *Bletter fun Mein Leben (Pages from My Life)*, Vol. III,
by Abraham Cahan, Forvertz Association, pp. 452–454

ZVI H. MASLIANSKY Addresses the Hebrew Union College in Hebrew, 1899

A venerated institution in Jewish life, now nearly extinct, was the *maggid* (preacher). The *maggid* was an itinerant sermonizer who attracted large audiences as he travelled through Russia, Poland, and even America. He used legends, folklore, parables, and imagery to enliven lectures dealing with religion, ethics, and, in later years, Zionism. Generally, he spoke on Shabbat afternoons in the synagogue.

In the United States, a *maggid* of the highest caliber was Zvi Hirsch Masliansky (1856–1943). He preached regularly at the Educational Alliance on East Broadway and drew capacity audiences. He was in great demand as a speaker everywhere. He began his career in Russia where he was caught up in the Love of Zion movement. In 1895, he came to the United States where he became known as one of Zion's greatest orators. His imposing appearance, learning, and brilliant delivery in Yiddish and Hebrew made him beloved among the immigrant generation. In 1899, he was invited to speak to the student body and faculty of the Hebrew Union College in Cincinnati.

"Study mikra *and you will counteract the waves of ignorance that engulf us. The dry* targum *... will fail to revive the Jewish spirit."*

I FOUND in Cincinnati two polarized communities—one strictly Orthodox, headed by two venerable rabbis and with daily study groups in *Talmud, Mishnah, Chaye Adam* [*Human Life,* important works on ethics and law], and Psalms which met between the afternoon and evening services. At the other extreme was the Reform Jewish community presided over by Dr. Isaac M. Wise, its founder and leader of the Hebrew Union College.

One of the college professors, Dr. Gotthard Deutch, a distinguished Hebrew scholar and historian, invited me, in behalf of Dr. Wise, to address the college body on the forthcoming Sabbath at the late afternoon services.

"But who will understand my talk which I shall have to give in Hebrew?" I asked.

"More than you think. Our professors, our Russian immigrant students, some of whom have studied at the Lithuanian *yeshivot* of Volozhin and Tels," he replied.

I accepted the invitation. Three students, the two brothers Jacob and Max Raisin [noted Hebraists and historians, then recent immigrants who upon graduation from HUC achieved prominence as rabbis and authors, who initiated the invitation] and Judah L. Magnes [see selections 26, 27, and 31] came to accompany me to the college.

At the college we were met by Drs. Wise and Deutch. The former was then about eighty years old, but he was sprightly like a man half his age. His face was animated, his eyes shone brightly, and his voice was clear and youthful. Dr. Deutch looked patriarchal, tall and handsome, with a large head, expansive brow, and a well-groomed, long beard. They led me to the chapel.

While going up the steps, Dr. Wise smilingly remarked to me, "I am thinking of the verse from Jeremiah which is appropriate for this occasion, 'I appoint you a prophet to the nations'" (1:5).

"No, Dr. Wise," I replied, "I am not a prophet and they are not *goyim* [a play on the Hebrew word for 'nations' which later became colloquial for Jews ignorant of their faith]."

"Then may I compromise by quoting a more suitable verse from Jeremiah, 'a messenger sent to the nations'" (49:14).

I smiled.

The chapel was filled to capacity. Besides the professors and students, a number of my newly acquired adherents from the community were present.

The services began with a responsive reading of Psalm 145 in English. Except for Dr. Deutch, who presided, and myself, the college body worshipped with their heads uncovered. One of the senior students removed a *Torah* scroll from the Holy Ark and unrolled it to the portion of the week (beginning with Genesis 37). He recited the opening blessing and dramatically read the first three verses. Then he recited the second blessing, rolled up the scroll, and stood it up on the pulpit.

Professor Deutch introduced me in Hebrew. He explained that I was not a Reform Jew, nor did I agree with the ideology of Reform Judaism, and that I was an Orthodox-nationalist Jew who preached and propagandized the ideas of Hibat Zion [the pre-Herzlian Zionist movement which sponsored the settlement of *Eretz Yisrael* by Jewish colonists]. He had read about me and he had heard me speak and was impressed with my oratorical talents and sincerity. Dr. Wise then invited me to address the college family.

I spoke in Hebrew for a full hour before an audience which was as strange to me as many of them were to Hebrew and my ideas. Speaking slowly and calmly, I described to them the suffering of our eight million brethren under the oppressive regime of the czar. I conveyed to them the sad yet inspiring story of their colleagues in the *yeshivot,* many of whom veritably make great sacrifices to study *Torah lishmah,* for its own sake, not as preparation for the rabbinate. . . . I made it clear that I did not come to debate with them about our ideological differences. But I asserted that I have a right to make one request of them, that they pursue diligently the study of *Torah* in the original, the study of Hebrew language and literature because they are the mainsprings of Judaism. I pleaded with them to counteract the spread of Jewish ignorance and indifference which spell extinction to our spiritual and moral life. I entreated them to observe the injunction of our sages that Jews should study the weekly *Torah* readings, two times in Hebrew (*shnayim mikra*) and once in translation (*echad targum*), and that I regretted to hear *targum* and noted the absence of *mikra*.

Reading the looks on the faces of my listeners that my message came through to them, I continued imploringly:

"Dear young colleagues, children of Abraham, Isaac, and Jacob, disciples of Isaiah, Hillel, and Johanan ben Zakkai, do you not feel my pain? A Jewish speaker has come to address you in a Jewish seminary in Hebrew and many cannot understand what he is saying. And some who do understand may wonder at the speaker's choice of language, as if Hebrew were a dead language like Greek or Latin. Study *mikra* and you will counteract the waves of ignorance that engulf us. The dry *targum* will not refresh the Jewish soul and will fail to revive the Jewish spirit."

Then turning to Dr. Wise, I exclaimed, "May I pour out my heart to you, our dear teacher. You know that last month, in Cleveland, one of your graduates, Rabbi G. [see postscript at the end of this selection], perpetrated a scandalous act which aroused bitter feelings among my Orthodox brethren and anger in the hearts of many in his temple. He removed the Holy Scroll from the Ark and relegated it to a secondary veiled resting place; in its sacred place he substituted for the weekly scriptural reading an English Bible."

My hands trembling and eyes filling with tears, I embraced the scroll which stood at my right. . . . "She [the word 'Torah' is feminine]was banished by one of your students. . . . You have brought us to this sad state with your extremist interpretation of Judaism."

I noticed two tears well up in the mild eyes of the old scholar and I said consolingly, "Forgive me, dear friend, for pouring out my aching heart to you. God is my witness that I did not mean to embarrass you."

Dr. Wise arose and extended his hand and with a silent gesture thanked me. When the service ended, many thanked me for my address. As I was leaving, Dr. Wise invited me and the brothers Raisin to his home. I readily assented. On his work table I saw Maimonides's *Mishneh Torah* [a code of law and ethics], Yehuda Ha Levi's *Kuzari* [a philosophic work], and the *Mikraot Gedolot* [the *Great Bible* with commentaries].

"Observe, my young and dear colleagues," he said, "how deeply you moved me. I invited you to see for yourself what works are always at my side. They are testimony to the fact that I am deeply attached to our Tradition. My heart, too, ached no less than yours when I heard of the wrongdoing of my former student. But the blame is not mine; it stems from Sinai in Chicago [Rabbi Emil G. Hirsch of Temple Sinai, Chicago, had substituted the English Scriptures for the *Torah*].

Suddenly he rose up and with his eyes aflame bade me to walk to the wall. As if hypnotized I, too, rose and walked to the wall.

"Further! Why do you not go on further?"

Bewildered, I replied, "I can't. The wall is in the way."

My host muttered sadly, "So it is with some of our foolish young people. They have gone far, too far, and have come up against a wall. Some have beaten their heads against it. But they will have to go back. I do not know if I shall live to see that day. I am past eighty; but you, dear friend, you will live to see it."

Translated from the Yiddish by the editor

From *Zichronos*, by Zvi Hirsch Masliansky,
Zerubavel Publisher, 1924, pp. 224-228

[Postscript:]

Dr. Jacob R. Marcus forwarded the above selection to Rabbi Daniel Jeremy Silver whose father, Abba Hillel, succeeded Rabbi G. and received this reply:

Dear Jacob:

Rabbi Gries suggested to the board that the *Torah* scroll be removed from the Ark. Presumably, because it was not read, he considered it an icon. The board, led by Abe Feder and Benjamin Lowenstein, opposed the change and it was never carried out. Interestingly, this episode led to the board's determination to seek a different kind of rabbi when Gries became ill in 1915.

D. J. S.

ELI GINZBERG Reflects on His Father's Contribution to the Jewish Encyclopedia, 1899

The turn of the century witnessed the rise of institutions which vitalized American Jewish culture. In 1892, the American Jewish Historical Society was founded, stimulating scholars to research and write on American Jewish history. The Jewish Theological Seminary was reorganized by Solomon Schechter in 1902 and became a citadel of rabbinic training and *Chochmat Yisrael* (Jewish Science). In 1909, Cyrus Adler led in the founding of Dropsie College in Philadelphia, a non-sectarian school for Semitic and Jewish studies. He also helped transfer the *Jewish Quarterly Review* from London to Philadelphia, where it has served as an outlet for Jewish and Semitic scholarly articles.

An event, the history of which has yet to be recorded, was the editing and publication (1900–1906) of the 12-volume illustrated *Jewish Encyclopedia,* acknowledged as the most comprehensive and scientific work of its kind. It attracted articles from the most outstanding world scholars. All of the subjects treated are of high excellence. Indeed, Jewish encyclopedias in Russian, Hebrew, German, and English that have appeared since drew freely from it.

The background and origin of the *Jewish Encyclopedia* were quite bizarre. Were it not for the fortuitous presence of Louis Ginzberg (1873–1953), a recent arrival and a rabbinic scholar (who later became the first faculty member of the Jewish Theological Seminary and served as professor of Talmud to the end of his days), the project would have turned out to be quite trivial. This is evidenced from the excerpts culled from the book *Keeper of the Law,* a memoir written by his son, Professor Eli Ginzberg, an outstanding economist, professor at Columbia University, and an authority in the field of human resources and human power. Incidentally, the selection which follows affords insights into the financial plight of the immigrant scholars and the struggle of the newly-organized Jewish Publication Society (and similar institutions) to establish itself.

"It is generally acknowledged that the Jewish Encyclopedia *. . . had no predecessor and to this day has had no true successor."*

"THE HEAD of the *Encyclopedia* was Isidore Singer, a second-rate journalist who was a native of Austria and had lived for many years in Paris. Actually, he came to the United States as an adventurer. His original idea was to incorporate in his encyclopedia the biographies of Jewish prize fighters and big businessmen. He thought that, if businessmen were approached and the proposal put to them that if they contributed five hundred dollars they would have half a page in the encyclopedia, and if they contributed one thousand dollars they would have a full page, the result would be a small fortune for himself. Singer had acquired his training and background through the 'revolver journalism' of Paris where prominent men, each of whom undoubtedly had some skeleton or other in his closet, would pay sums of money to keep the gossip out of the paper. The other way the journals and journalists amassed money was to promise the *nouveaux riches* that their soirees, etc., would be fully reported—for certain considerations. Funk and Wagnalls was the publisher of the *Encyclopedia.* Dr. Funk was a very shrewd man; he recognized the possibility of getting very large funds from the Jews and proceeded to do so." [The words within quotation marks throughout this selection are those of Professor Louis Ginzberg.]

So much for the background of the undertaking. How did Louis Ginzberg come into contact with the promoters? "I started to work with the *Encyclopedia* purely by accident. Their building was on Lafayette Street, which was then right next to the public library. I had met Singer and others who suggested that I drop into the *Encyclopedia* office. When I did, I apparently impressed the editors when I picked up a piece of paper on which was written a list of proposed names and subjects. The compilers had copied from French and German and other sources, which made for a duplication of titles. On one page, I found 25 repetitions. Kohler [Professor Kaufmann Kohler (1843–1926), president of Hebrew Union College (1903–1921), scholar, and leader of Reform Jewry] suggested that I write some articles for them and we were off."

Rabbi Marcus Jastrow, who was the head of a large congregation in Philadelphia and who, in addition to his career as minister, pursued scholarly investigations, was in charge of the Rabbinical Department of the *Encyclopedia*. The articles prepared by young Ginzberg, who was at first paid by the piece, so impressed Jastrow that he recommended to the Board of Editors that primary responsibility be transferred from himself to Ginzberg who clearly had the greater knowledge. This generous act by an older man smoothed Ginzberg's way. He was soon on the regular payroll, writing on a wide range of subjects and receiving a salary of $25 per week, approximately the same that he would have earned at the Hebrew Union College.

Singer may have had many weaknesses, but he was clearly able to excite the enthusiasm of outstanding people and to elicit their cooperation. The Editorial Board of the *Encyclopedia* was composed of most of the Jewish scholars in the United States, many of whom, like Kaufmann Kohler and Marcus Jastrow, were also busy rabbis. It was a lively and hardworking group, and it is difficult to think of a better environment for a newly arrived young scholar to get his American land legs.

My father must have found the environment very congenial, for his output was prodigious. In the two years that he was with them, his initials were signed to 234 articles under the letter "A," with almost another 100 under the letter "B"; altogether he prepared a total of 406 articles. While many were brief biographies, several were of monograph length and three stood the test of time sufficiently to be reprinted in a volume of his collected essays, *On Jewish Law and Lore*, more than a half century later: "Allegorical Interpretation of Scripture"; "The Cabbala: History and System"; and "Codification of Jewish Law."

It is generally acknowledged that the *Jewish Encyclopedia* that Singer promoted and to which my father contributed so much had no predecessor and to this day has had no true successor. There have been many Jewish encyclopedias in the intervening decades, but even the best of them have borrowed indiscriminately from the *Jewish Encyclopedia* of the early 1900s, the product of an unsuccessful promoter, a shrewd publisher, generous laymen, and an intrepid band of scholars and writers, among whom Louis Ginzberg came to play a key role.

By the time the first volume was completed and published, in 1900, Funk and Wagnalls had invested at least $50,000 in the venture. My father recalled that "the general press as well as the Jewish press, of course, received the first volume enthusiastically, and it was after all a very respectable achievement. The company gave a dinner for the editors and the first volume was launched with enthusiasm and acclaim. But Dr. Funk said that his company could no longer afford to continue the undertaking. He said that he would rather lose all of the money already invested than to pour more money into a bad venture. By this time, wealthy and influential Jews were becoming interested, and immediately offers of assistance poured in. Mr. Schiff promised to buy a large number of sets. But work on the *Encyclopedia* prematurely stopped." Louis Ginzberg was earning $60 a week by this time, a very nice salary indeed, but he was restive about what the future held in store. He was afraid that Kohler might try to retrench in a manner that would inevitably jeopardize the scholarly standards that the first volume had set. . . .

He early made the acquaintance of two of America's foremost Semitics scholars, George Foot Moore of Harvard and Charles Torrey of Yale. During the Easter vacation of 1900, the Oriental Society of America met in Philadelphia and Moore and Torrey said "that it would be a good idea for me to come to Philadelphia to get acquainted with some of these people. After all, the *Jewish Encyclopedia* job might not last forever. Judge Mayer Sulzberger learned about my being in town and came to pay me a visit. (He was lucky to find me. I had registered at a hotel near the station and had gone off to another where the meetings were being held. That night found me wandering in and out of a series of hotels looking at the registers for a friend whose name I was ostensibly seeking, while in fact I searched for my own signature.) Later, I spent a whole day with Sulzberger from 11 A.M. to 11 P.M. at his home."

My father had the highest regard for Sulzberger. . . . "In a certain sense, Sulzberger was the most genuine American Jew I ever met. He was a bachelor; he was a collector; he had an extraordinary fine literary style—he could be a professor of English at any university; he was a leading jurist of the day, probably he was the best-known citizen of Philadelphia. He was Judge of Common Pleas and a man of great integrity among men of little integrity. He was a unique personality. He had a Jewish background in life and thought. He knew Jewish life by living it, not by reading about it. He was a man of action and a man of vision. Take, for instance, his idea that we should have a fine Jewish library in America. He came to this conclusion before any institution of Jewish learning had such an idea. He helped build the nucleus of the library which is now at the Jewish Theological Seminary. Three years after my arrival in this country, one of the richest private libraries in the world was sold in Amsterdam. Sulzberger cabled orders directly to my father, and he continued to buy manuscripts and rare books."

The advice given by Moore and Torrey proved to be sensible.

The *Encyclopedia* job did not last forever. My father found himself employed on a week-to-week basis, an unsatisfactory arrangement. He gave serious consideration to returning to Europe. He talked about this to Sulzberger who said, "You would be the first man of ability to go back. If America can't do anything, Europe certainly can't. Something will turn up." To help bridge the gap until the *Encyclopedia* would again go full throttle ahead or an academic post could be found for him, Sulzberger suggested that my father write a small popular volume of Jewish legends which the Jewish Publication Society could publish. Since he had worked with legendary materials both in connection with his doctoral dissertation and in connection with his many assignments for the *Encyclopedia*, this suggestion . . . was attractive.

The terms of the agreement have been preserved in a letter from Henrietta Szold, the secretary of the Society [JPS], to my father, dated November 6, 1901:

> Your letter of September 18 submitting [your] plan for the proposed work on "Jewish Legends Relating to Biblical Matters" was put before the Publication Committee by the chairman early in October and by it approved and recommended for adoption to the Board of Trustees. The latter has now had its meeting, and I am instructed to write you that your proposition has been accepted, together with the terms you suggest. The understanding is that you will write, in German, a book, on the lines laid down in your proposition, to contain approximately one hundred thousand words and to be available for use of the Society in the year 1903, all rights in the book to be ceded to the Jewish Publication Society of America for an honorarium of $1,000.
>
> The Committee suggests that, as the manuscript must be handled by a translator, it be written in ink and only on one side of the paper.

Agreements are usually entered in good faith, but here is proof, if proof be needed, of how fate and time can alter the plans of men—and women. No volume was made available for the use of the Society in 1903, nor in the next year, or the year following. The first volume of what eventually came to be a seven-volume work entitled *The Legends of the Jews* appeared in 1909. It was not until 1913 that the fourth volume of text appeared. And it was more than a decade later in 1925 that the first volume of the notes was published, followed three years later by the second volume of the notes. And still many more years passed before the appearance of the Index Volume because those guiding the Society were apprehensive about the expense and failed to realize that it would soon more than pay for itself, since it would unlock the treasures that were contained in the six volumes that had been published earlier, particularly the volumes containing the notes.

We cannot help wondering in light of what happened whether Miss Szold was prescient in recommending to the author to write in ink and on only one side of the paper in order to lighten the task of the translator; she herself translated the first two volumes.

Sulzberger's gambit was succeeded beyond his wildest dreams. Although the Jewish Publication Society had to wait a long time for the volume that had been promised for 1903, it eventually had the distinction of publishing one of the most important studies ever written on the folkloristic materials of the Bible. The gambit was also successful in its primary aim: It helped to keep Louis Ginzberg in America.

At the end of about three-quarters of a year of shrewd negotiations between Dr. Funk and the leadership of the American Jewish community, the money was in hand to proceed with the original plan and to bring out a comprehensive encyclopedia which would be distinguished for its authoritative treatment of every significant aspect of Jewish life and letters in ancient, medieval, and modern times.

Work resumed and Louis Ginzberg returned to his editorial duties. The volume of legends to which he had recently committed himself had to be put aside. It is interesting to record my father's picture of Dr. Funk who played such a determining role in this most ambitious publishing undertaking. "Funk was a Lutheran minister who was very active in the temperance movement. He was at one time the Prohibition party's candidate for vice-president. One day he invited me to lunch at the Astor, then the swankiest hotel in town. I knew he was a temperance man. Our waiter—all of the waiters were German—asked me what I would drink. I said that I would start with a glass of Bordeaux and end with a cognac. Funk just sat there trembling; he couldn't say a word. Finally, I said I *would* drink that, but my doctor says that I shouldn't, so I will just have water.

"I had an office in a building which was next to the public library on Eighth Street. I rarely worked in the office. I preferred to work in the library. Funk asked me what I was doing spending so much time in the library. I told him that I was just disarranging books. . . ."

Some time later my father was introduced to the mightiest of them all—Jacob H. Schiff—perhaps the wealthiest Jew in the United States and the self-appointed as well as generally acknowledged head of American Jewry. Without much general or Jewish learning, Schiff nevertheless had been brought up in a sufficiently Jewish world in Frankfurt-am-Main that he sought to discharge his responsibilities both with regard to supporting his brethren in need and to building and supporting Jewish institutions that would contribute to their religious and cultural life. He was a philanthropist on the grand scale.

From *Keeper of the Law*, by Eli Ginzberg,
1966, pp. 65–77. Reprinted by permission of the publisher,
the Jewish Publication Society of America

A CHRISTIAN JOURNALIST Views
Jewish Life on the East Side, 1900

There was no question to the general observer that
Jewish family life on the East Side was deteriorating
rapidly. Parents could not adjust to the booming, buzz-
ing confusion around them. Preoccupied with eking
out a bare living, they did not pay heed to their
children to try to create a life style suitable to the New
World. They spoke languages different from those
of their children who lived in conflicting cultures.
The Old World filial respect for parents gave way to
alienation and scorn. Parents felt helpless; the future
looked bleak indeed.

Of course, we know that this was only an episode
in the unfolding history of the Jews. Jewish resilience
and *élan vital* (original life force) soon asserted themselves. But to Lincoln Steffens (1866–1936), the break-
up that he witnessed touched him deeply. A journalist
par excellence, he is best known for his work, *The
Shame of the Cities,* in which he exposed the corrup-
tion and vice in municipal governments at the turn of
the century. He was among the first of the muckrakers
in American journalism.

Steffens, a Christian, was introduced to Jewish life
by another reporter, Abe Cahan (see selection 13).
He fell in love with the Old World Jews and endeav-
ored to become one of them, without actually convert-
ing to Judaism. The passage which follows is taken
from his celebrated autobiography.

"Two, three thousand years of continuous devotion,
courage, and suffering for a cause lost in a generation."

I SOON FOUND OUT that by going with the reporters to a
fire or the scene of an accident was a way to see the town and
the life of the town.

A synagogue that burned down during a service introduced
me to the service; I attended another synagogue, asked questions, and realized that it was a bit of the Old Testament repeated after thousands of years, unchanged. And so I described
that service and other services. They fascinated me, those old
practices, and the picturesque customs and laws of the old Orthodox Jews from Russia and Poland. . . . I read up and talked to
funny old, fine rabbis about them and about their conflicts with
their Americanized children. The *Post* observed all the holy days
of the ghetto. There were advance notices of their coming, with
descriptions of the preparations and explanations of their sacred
ancient, biblical meaning, and then an account of them as I saw
[them] observed in the homes and the synagogues. . . . A queer
mixture of comedy, tragedy, orthodoxy, and revelation, they interested our Christian readers. The uptown Jews complained now
and then. Mr. Godkin himself required me once to call personally upon a socially prominent Jewish lady who had written to
the editor asking why so much space was given to the ridiculous
performances of the ignorant, foreign East Side Jews and none to
the uptown Hebrews. I told her. I had the satisfaction of telling
her about the comparative beauty, significance, and character of
the uptown and downtown Jews. I must have talked well for she
threatened and tried to have me fired, as she put it. Fortunately,
the editorial writers were under pressure also from prominent
Jews to back up their side of a public controversy over the black-
balling of a rich Jew by an uptown social club. "We" were fair
to the Jews, editorially, but personally irritated. I was not "fired";
I was sent out to interview the proprietor of a hotel which excluded Jews, and he put his case in a very few words.

"I won't have one," he said. "I have had my experience and so learned that, if you let one in because he is exceptional and fine, he will bring others who are not exceptional, etc. By and by they will occupy the whole house when the Christians leave. And then, when the Christians don't come any more, the Jews quit you to go where the Christians have gone, and there you are with an empty or a second-class house."

It would have been absurd to discharge me since I at that time was almost a Jew. I had become as infatuated with the ghetto as eastern boys were with the Wild West and nailed a *mezuzah* on my office door; I went to the synagogue on all the great Jewish holy days; on *Yom Kippur* I spent the whole twenty-four hours fasting and going from one synagogue to another. The music moved me most, but I knew and could follow with the awful feelings of a Jew the beautiful old ceremonies of the ancient Orthodox services. My friends laughed at me; especially the Jews among them scoffed. "You are more Jewish than us Jews," they said, and since I have travelled I realize the absurdity of the American who is more French than the French, more German than the Kaiser. But there were some respecters of my respect. When Israel Zangwill, the author of *Tales of the Ghetto,* came from London to visit New York, he heard about me from Jews and asked me to be his guide for a survey of the East Side; and he saw and he went home and wrote *The Melting Pot.*

The tales of the New York ghetto were heartbreaking comedies of the tragic conflict between the old and the new, the very old and the very new; in many matters, all at once: religion, class, clothes, manners, customs, language, culture. We all know the difference between youth and age, but our experience is between two generations. Among the Russian and other Eastern Jewish families in New York it was an abyss of many generations; it was between parents out of the Middle Ages, sometimes out of the Old Testament days hundreds of years B.C., and the children of the streets of New York today [1900]. We saw it everywhere all the time. Responding to a reported suicide, we would pass a synagogue where a score or more of boys were sitting hatless in their old clothes, smoking cigarettes on the steps outside, and their fathers, all dressed in black, with their high hats, uncut beards, and side curls, were going into the synagogues, tearing their hair and rending their garments. The reporters stopped to laugh; and it was comic; the old men, in their thrift, tore the lapels of their coats very carefully, a very little, but they wept tears, real tears. It was a revolution. Their sons were rebels against the Law of Moses; they were lost souls, lost to God, the family, and to Israel of old. The police did not understand or sympathize. If there was a fight—and sometimes the fathers did lay hands on their sons, and the tough boys did biff their fathers in the eye; which brought out all the horrified elders of the whole neighborhood and all the sullen youth—when there was a "riot call," the police would rush in and club now the boys, now the parents, and now, in their Irish exasperation, both sides, bloodily and in vain. I used to feel that blood did not hurt, but the tears did, the weeping and gnashing of teeth of the old Jews who were doomed and knew it. Two, three thousand years of continuous devotion, courage, and suffering for a cause lost in a generation.

From *The Autobiography of Lincoln Steffens,*
Harcourt Brace and Co., 1931, pp. 243–245

LOUIS BORGENICHT Rises in the Business World, 1900

Louis Borgenicht (1861–1942) came to this country, in 1888 at the age of 27, with his wife Regina. During the earlier part of his life, he was a comparatively modest businessman. His story typifies the rise of a poor immigrant, in the children's dress industry, through ambition, perseverance, integrity, and a talent for original ideas.

In this country, Borgenicht started out as a pushcart peddler selling herring. Dissatisfied, but eager to better his condition, he decided to manufacture children's aprons which he had seen worn in Europe but not in New York. He bought 150 yards of gingham plus trimming; his wife agreed to be his seamstress. In a few days he was in business! In three hours he had sold all the aprons at a small profit of $2.60.

One idea led to another. The next step was to manufacture children's dresses. Again, Regina helped. Some samples were sold to well-known stores such as Macy's, Gimbels, and Bloomingdale's. But Borgenicht was still far from the success he desired.

In the following excerpt, Borgenicht relates, in his own words, the beginning of his climb to success.

"Everything is as you said, down to the last 'T'."

FOR ME three events marked the year that followed [1900]. . . . The three things were close to home. . . .

In that year I opened up the piece-goods "commission houses" . . . to what is known as the "cut-up" trade.

A commission house is a sales organization which contracts

with a mill to sell the entire product of the looms and to take all the credit risks involved in return for a commission. . . . The commission houses sold only in big lots to jobbers from whom, in turn, the manufacturer had to buy his smaller lots of goods. . . .

One day I realized that, if I could manage to buy directly from Lawrence & Company . . . one of the most important mills . . . , I could cut out the jobber's profit and produce my goods for that much less. A simple proposition—but it was novel. . . .

Brash, and perhaps naively so, I visited Mr. Bingham, the all-important credit man of Lawrence & Company. I took one look at this tall, gaunt, whitebearded Yankee with the steel blue eyes and knew that I would like to deal with him. I made my proposal bluntly. . . . I wanted to buy forty cases of cashmeres directly. . . . I would pay cash on delivery, in three shipments.

Bingham sat holding a pen in his hand and staring at me from under raised, bristling eyebrows.

"You have a h--- of a cheek coming in here and asking me for favors!" he said. "Why should I do it?"

. . . I launched into an explanation of my position and prospects. Honest, hardworking, dealing with fine customers, I was a cinch to make good if Bingham would help me. . . .

Bingham stroked his long white beard as he listened. When I had finished . . . he looked at me without apparent enthusiasm.

"You still have a h--- of a cheek," he said—and then he smiled. "We'll do it!"

That simple speech was, to my knowledge, the first break in the solid front of the commission houses. The sale . . . was their first direct transaction with the cut-up trade. . . . For the fledgling industry it was a tremendous advance. . . .

The second event . . . was the inventory we took on February 1, 1900. It was long after midnight when I came home. Regina was asleep, but I had to wake her. . . .

"Ma, I have news for you," I whispered, so as not to wake the children. "Wonderful news!"

"You and your news!" she shrugged and lay down again.

"But it is great news," I insisted. "We have made a profit of ten thousand dollars!"

"*Zehn tausend dollar!*"

It was a colossal sum. . . . Starting with absolutely nothing, I had made in one year a net profit of ten thousand dollars!

Next day we reached the third milestone. The morning mail brought a letter from a . . . salesman for [a] competitor. . . . This Mr. Simon had approached the Boston Store in Chicago only to be told that . . . they were making all their purchases from a little man on East Broadway. This merchandise was beautiful, they said, and it sold like lemonade on a hot summer's day. . . . They had advised him to try . . . [to] connect with the newcomer, Borgenicht. "Get his line and we'll give you our business. . . ."

The proposition Simon offered was that he would represent me in the larger western cities, working on a commission basis to be paid after the goods were sold. No drawing, no expense for me at all!

At about the same time I heard from a salesman in San Francisco, a city of whose existence I had hardly been aware. . . . A Stockton, California, buyer had come all the way . . . over to my East Side place to look over my line—in itself an unprecedented event—and had almost cleared my shelves. Returning to the West Coast, he had advised his salesman friend to write to me. The salesman . . . wanted to transfer to my staff as agent for the Far West.

Both these offers I had to decline. . . . I could only promise to inform these correspondents as soon as my capital and production facilities were adequate. . . . But . . . these letters bowled me over. That I should be in a position even to think of a representative in San Francisco! I had to get used to the idea gradually. I have never lost the thrill it gave me. . . .

Lawrence & Company had already sold [to] me for cash. Now I went up to tackle the proposition of purchasing on credit. That would enable me to treble my business. . . . I put forward a concrete offer of a twenty-five thousand-dollar order. . . .

"How will you pay for the goods?" asked Bingham curiously.

"When the bill falls due, I'll pay it!"

"And what makes you think I'll extend the credit?"

"When I explain my position," I replied with apparent confidence, "I'm sure you will!"

I presented my case. I understood my line thoroughly. . . . Hardworking and honest, I was anxious not only to support my family but also to prove myself worthy of the citizenship papers I had taken out in the country which I had chosen, deliberately and not by accident of birth. Finally, I added, I was prepared to sign a statement of my financial status in black on white, with the understanding that Bingham would come up to my lofts to check it for himself. If my statement deviated by one hair from what he found, I would let him kick me out of his office personally. If, on the other hand, he found that everything tallied, I wanted him for a friend. . . .

"Grant me this one favor," I begged Bingham, "and I will remember it for a lifetime!"

On a hot July day . . . he walked suddenly into my office. Within five minutes his coat was off and his blue eyes were peering into my books. For three hours . . . [he] roamed through the place like a hungry tiger, poking into every corner. Finishing with the books, he jotted down a few figures of his own, then [he] stalked through the raw materials and the ready dresses. He thumbed . . . our lists of customers, nodding over the names. . . .

When he was quite through, beads of perspiration stood out on his high forehead under his white hair. His face flushed, . . . he stretched out a massive fist.

"Borgenicht, let's shake hands," he boomed. "Everything is as you said, down to the last 'T'. Buy what you need and when you need it. The house is open to you. . . ."

From *The Happiest Man: The Life of Louis Borgenicht*,
by Harold Friedman, Putnam's, 1942, pp. 251–256

SOLOMON SCHECHTER Serves as President of Jewish Theological Seminary, 1902-1915

In 1887, the Jewish Theological Seminary (the school for training Conservative rabbis and educators) was opened in the vestry rooms of the Spanish and Portuguese Synagogue (Shearith Israel) in New York (see Part One, selection 11). Lacking the necessary facilities and finances as well as suitable faculty and library, it was soon apparent that unless it was reorganized it would founder.

Community-spirited Jewish leaders began to search for a scholar of stature to head the school, set up a faculty, erect a building, and attract a board of trustees befitting a rabbinical institution. Spearheading this effort were Reform Jewish leaders who supported the Hebrew Union College.

Jacob H. Schiff financed the erection of a building on West 123rd Street, adjacent to Columbia University, and gave generously to acquire library collections from famous European Jewish scholars. Louis Marshall agreed to serve as chairman of the Board of Trustees.

In 1902, Rumanian-born Solomon Schechter resigned his position as teacher at Cambridge University, England, to assume the presidency of the JTS. His arrival at these shores marked the rise of the seminary and the growth of the Conservative movement. Schechter had achieved world fame for bringing to light some 100,000 manuscripts, documents, and fragments which were hidden away in the *genizah* (a repository of ancient documents, fragments of sacred scrolls, and books which, because they contain the Holy Name of God, were hidden away or buried) in the attic of the old Cairo synagogue. These priceless treasures revealed about five hundred years of hitherto

Congregation Shearith Israel whose vestry rooms housed the first
Jewish Theological Seminary. (American Jewish Archives)

unknown aspects of Jewish life and culture in Baby-
lonia, the Orient, and early medieval Europe. Only the
discovery of the Dead Sea Scrolls, in the caves of
Qumran in the Judean Desert in 1947, outranked the
genizah discoveries.

Schechter believed in the future of American Jewry.
He captured the interest of diverse segments in the
Jewish community. He attracted outstanding scholars
to serve on the faculty; established an institute to train
generations of Hebrew teachers for American Jewish
religious schools; inspired the organization of the
Rabbinical Assembly for ordained Conservative rabbis;
developed the United Synagogue of America and its
constituents; and laid the groundwork for the JTS
library, one of the most outstanding collections in the
Western Hemisphere.

Following the teaching of Kohelet, "Cast your bread
upon the waters for you will find it after many days"
(Ecclesiastes 11:1), a comparatively unknown modest
but wealthy man named Louis Brush was so impressed by Solomon Schechter and his wife, Mathilde,
that he bequeathed his fortune which made possible
the present buildings of the Jewish Theological Seminary on Broadway and 122nd Street, housing the
seminary, the Teachers Institute, the library, and
dormitories. The Rabbinical Assembly and the United
Synagogue of America grew in numbers and impor-
tance and, in time, led in the campaign to raise the
budget for the Seminary.

Schechter's influence transcended the Jewish Theological Seminary and the Conservative movement. He
was a central figure in the growth of the Jewish Publication Society, the editing of the new translation of
the Holy Scriptures, and the *Jewish Quarterly Review*.

However, during the late years of his life, Solomon
Schechter had become discouraged and weary. To
him, Jewish learning was paramount. He was unhappy
and jealous of the interest, time, and support which
the seminary directors gave to other communal causes.
Some of the heaviness of spirit of those years is revealed in a memorandum, sent on December 13, 1913,

to Louis Marshall, chairman of the Board of Trustees, which is reproduced here.

"My main reason for giving up such an ideal life . . . was the conviction that the future of Israel was in America. . . ."

. . . WHEN I RECEIVED the call in Cambridge to come over and take charge of the Seminary, I understood that the purpose of the institution was a twofold one. First, to establish a training school for rabbis which, adopting what is best in modern thought but at the same time teaching traditional Judaism in such a manner as to awaken fresh interest in our glorious past, should create a Conservative school removed alike from both extremes, Radical-Reform and Hyper-Orthodoxy. . . . Secondly, to inaugurate a school of higher Jewish learning which, applying the best academic methods to the various departments of Hebrew literature, should create in this country a home for original research worthy of taking its place by the side of academic institutions of a similar character as they were created by European Jewry during the last century. . . . It was the intention that this college should be endowed in such a way as to make it entirely independent of all outside opinion so that it could pursue its way on the lines mapped out for it without any fear of interference. . . . I still remember the favourable reception shown to my first report. I spoke there of a large faculty, of publications, of scholarships or fellowships, of frequent intercourse between the directors, the faculty, and students, of a large library, and of a good staff for the library. . . .

And these ideals were realized to a large extent. The average number of graduates from the Seminary was five a year, the majority of whom are now occupying pulpits in Conservative congregations. If a small minority has forsaken the Conservative cause and accepted calls from Reform pulpits, it is owing to the terrible conditions under which the Conservative rabbi has to labour. . . . But the Conservative influence was not confined to our students. It extended also to the Reform section of the community which fell under its spell and began to look at Judaism from a point of view differing widely from that prevalent before. When I came here I remember that one of our trustees said to me: "Your work must not finish within the walls of the Seminary. It will be your mission also to reform the Reformers." And I think that everyone familiar with the conditions both in the East and in the West will readily admit that this hope was largely realized.

Not less were our hopes realized as regards Jewish learning. It is no exaggeration to say that the last ten years saw more books of the substantial learned order published by American Jewish scholars than all the two hundred years and more since Israel began to dwell in this country. . . . American Jewish scholarship is now a fact which is recognized and appreciated all over the world, both by Jews and Christians. . . .

It should also be recorded that the Seminary has its full share in the religious educational movement. It was the Seminary which first drew attention to the lack of religious education and properly trained teachers. It also inaugurated a regular teacher's course in which instruction to many pupils was given. This work is now carried on by our graduates who, wherever they come, establish Sabbath schools or *Talmud Torahs,* conducted in a methodical and systematic way.

Thus, the Seminary proved a factor for good in American Israel, though its work is not of the sensational kind. And what it has done it has accomplished in the teeth of many opposing forces which, in former years, were attacking it on all possible occasions. Indeed, whilst all the sections of the community, whether Orthodox or Reform, have their organs singing their praises of the party to which they belong and making constantly proselytes for their cause, the Seminary was entirely dependent on its own work to reach the public. . . .

But I cannot help thinking that the Seminary is given little credit for what it has accomplished. And, instead of encouraging it to follow on the path it had set out, there is an unmistakable tendency to reproach us for our want of forming large constituencies and enlisting the support and the goodwill of what is described as the "Orthodox public." It is overlooked that an institution which is meant to pursue a middle course and to create new currents of thought and action could not possibly be popular with the crowd whose mind is, as a rule, given to extremes and to radical action, whether Orthodox or Reform. It is further forgotten that no institution of higher learning could ever expect the support of the people.

. . . I hate to speak of myself. But matters, unfortunately, have reached such a pass that I must touch on the personal question. Every Englishman connected either with the University or with the Jewish community will bear witness to the fact that my position in Cambridge was a most satisfactory one. I enjoyed there a reputation as a scholar, which was constantly growing. With the exception of two hours a week, my time was fully given up to the pursuit of my own studies. My main reason for giving up such an ideal life and so eminently suited for a student was the conviction that the future of Israel was in America and that it was the very country, if anywhere, in which it was necessary that some great centre of Jewish learning and Conservative activity should be created. It was the hope of being in some way instrumental in creating such a centre, and the fair assurance of absolute independence indispensable for such a creation, that prevailed with me in the end. But I must frankly say that no consideration in the world would ever have induced me, in my comparatively advanced age, to leave the precincts of Cambridge had I known that the Seminary was largely meant for a particular section of the community, forming a sort of higher *Talmud Torah*, having the purpose of reconciling the most unruly element in Jewry and giving it a little religious refinement. It is true that I never heard such a sentiment expressed by the board, but the growing indifference on the part of several of the trustees of the institution makes me believe that I am not quite wrong in my judgement. . . .

I fully appreciate the magnanimity and sacrifice brought by some of our trustees for the institution. But I feel not less humiliated by the indifference of others. I am sorry to speak in such frank language. But my experience within the last four or five years was one continuous mortification to me, which was calculated to make the last few years of my life a period of constant care and anxiety. It is a terrible thing to see one's hopes and aspirations shattered to pieces. For I cannot help feeling that the Seminary is in a sadly struggling condition. . . . An appeal to the public at large is of little use and, as far as my experience goes, such appeals have only done us harm and injury. Relief, therefore, can only be expected from the trustees, and it is their sympathy and interest which I endeavour to enlist anew in this memorandum.

From *Solomon Schechter: A Biography*, by Norman Bentwich,
1938, pp. 191–195. Copyright © by the publisher,
the Jewish Publication Society of America

OSCAR S. STRAUS Details the Protests of President Theodore Roosevelt and America against the Kishinev Pogroms. 1903

On February 16, 1903, a Christian boy was found murdered near Kishinev in the Russian province of Bessarabia. (It was revealed later that the assassin was a relative who wanted to get part of the fortune the boy would inherit.) For two months the Russian government and church fomented anti-Semitic agitation, accusing the Jews of killing the boy in order to use his blood for Passover *matzah*. (This was the age-old blood libel.) The campaign was carefully manipulated so as to culminate in wide-ranging pogroms during the Christian Easter holidays (the "open season" for pogroms). In the riots of April 19–20, 1903, which affected 2,750 Jewish families, 47 were killed and nearly 100 were injured. Jewish property valued at about $1,250,000 was destroyed and pillaged; women were raped; and other atrocities were perpetrated.

In those days the world was much more sensitized to evil than it was thirty years later when the Hitler era began. Protests by Jews and non-Jews were worldwide. The press, church, and synagogue, as well as governmental and civic agencies, denounced the Russian government and the perpetrators of the pogroms. Demonstrations and protest rallies were held in many cities. The excerpt which follows is from the reminiscences of Oscar S. Straus (1850–1926), a prominent American public official who was the first Jew to serve in a presidential cabinet. He was secretary of Commerce and Labor under Theodore Roosevelt.

"Official Russia was made to realize the aroused indignation . . . of the civilized world."

IN NEW YORK a mass meeting was called at Carnegie Hall, by hundreds of the foremost New York Christians, in protest against the outrages upon the Jews in Russia and particularly against the Kishinev affair. The speakers were ex-President [Grover] Cleveland, Mayor Seth Low, Jacob G. Schurman, president of Cornell. . . . I have in my possession the manuscript of Cleveland's address on this occasion, which concludes:

"In the meantime, let the people of the United States, gathered together in such assemblages as this in every part of the land, fearlessly speak to the civilized world—protesting against every pretense of civilization that permits medieval persecution, against every bigoted creed that forbids religious toleration and freedom of conscience, against all false enlightenment that excuses hatred and cruelty towards any race of man, and against all spurious forms of government protection that withhold from any human being the right to live in safety and toil in peace."

I will also quote part of the resolutions adopted that evening:

"Resolved, that the people of the United States should exercise such influence with the government of Russia, as the ancient and unbroken friendship between the two nations may justify, to stay the spirit of persecution, to redress the injuries inflicted upon the Jews of Kishinev, and to prevent the recurrence of outbreaks such as have amazed the civilized world."

A few weeks later a committee from the B'nai B'rith Order . . . headed by their president, Leo N. Levi, called upon Secretary of State John Hay and presented to him a statement regarding the massacres . . . together with a proposed petition which they wished forwarded to the government of the czar. The Secretary expressed great sympathy and the desire to do what might be possible in the matter. His reply to the committee, taken down in shorthand at the time, was published in full in the press, and from it I quote the concluding sentence:

"All we know of the state of things in Russia tends to justify the hope that even out of the present terrible situation some good results may come; that He who watches over Israel does not slumber."

The Secretary then accompanied the committee to the White House where they met the President and presented to him an outline of the oppression of their coreligionists in Russia.

Early in July, I received a telegram from the President's secretary to the effect that the President would like to have me lunch with him the day following at Oyster Bay and that Simon Wolf of Washington and Leo N. Levi also had been invited. . . .

We discussed the Russian situation throughout lunch. The President suggested that a note be sent by the Secretary of State to John W. Riddle, our charge at St. Petersburg, and that this note should embody the entire petition which Mr. Levi and his committee had drafted. . . . The petition to the czar and giving publicity to the note would have all the effects of a presentation even if the czar should refuse to receive it. . . .

After luncheon we adjourned to the study, and Roosevelt said: "Now let's finish this thing up." Hay had been to see him the day before and had left a memorandum. Roosevelt at once drafted the note with his own pen, using part of Hay's memorandum. The note was to be sent as an open cable. It read as follows:

Riddle
St. Petersburg

You are instructed to ask an audience of the Minister of Foreign Affairs and to make to him the following communication:

Excellency: The Secretary of State instructs me to inform you that the President has received from a large number of prominent citizens of the United States of all religious affiliations, and occupying the highest positions in both public and private life, a respectful petition addressed to His Majesty the Emperor relating to the condition of the Jews in Russia and running as follows: [Here is set out the petition.]

I am instructed to ask whether the petition will be received by Your Excellency to be submitted to the gracious consideration of His Majesty. In that case the petition will be at once forwarded to St. Petersburg.

Roosevelt wanted the cable to be sent at once and was in a hurry to get it to Washington. . . . The President asked whether I could take it so that it might be dispatched next morning. By ten o'clock the following morning I placed the draft in the Secretary's hands and it was immediately put on the wire.

In planning the cable as he did, the President was right in his anticipation. Duly the American charge at St. Petersburg informed the State Department that the Russian government, through its Minister of Foreign Affairs, had declined to receive or consider the petition. Nevertheless, its purpose was accomplished. Official Russia was made to realize the aroused indignation and the public protests of the civilized world. This in turn had a decided influence in checking, for the time being at least, similar outbreaks threatened throughout the empire, besides bringing to trial and punishment some of the leaders of the massacres.

From *Under Four Administrations*, by Oscar S. Straus,
Houghton Mifflin, 1922, pp. 169–173

DAVID BLAUSTEIN, Director of the Educational Alliance, Surveys the Lower East Side, 1904

The Educational Alliance, on East Broadway at the corner of Jefferson Street in New York City, was an outstanding Jewish agency for Americanization. Founded by German Jews, it was originally called the Hebrew Institute and nicknamed the "Palace of Immigrants." However, to eliminate sectarian implications, the name was changed to the Educational Alliance. It became a second home to many East Side Jews, young and old. It provided classes in English and the arts, a library and reading room, athletics, and recreation and entertainment of all types. Immigrants were taught how to salute the American flag and celebrate American holidays and to sing national songs. At first, Yiddish had been prohibited in the building; hence, most of the ghetto Jews went their own way, ignoring classes, clubs, and activities. Yiddish-speaking, they were, in the main, oriented to trade unionism and socialism. The Orthodox and synagogue-minded sent their children to Hebrew schools. The Yiddish press and theater struck deep roots and actively competed for their interest.

It was evident that the greenhorn was not a *tabula rasa*, a blank page to be filled in. So the Educational Alliance adapted its policy to accommodate and attract them. The trustees replaced the incumbent director with a new man, David Blaustein, an East European Jew who had served as rabbi but was trained in social work as well. In a short time he became a central figure on the East Side. One of his first projects was to survey the Alliance's field of service.

". . . The total amount paid out in this neighborhood
for instruction amounts to $10,000 a month. . . ."

LADIES AND GENTLEMEN: . . . I took a census of the Lower
East Side which takes in about 32 streets south of Houston
Street and east of the Bowery. . . . I will simply give you an idea
of what is to be found in this square mile.

There are 5,000 tenements, with 64,268 families. Of these . . .
6,499 persons have 84 different occupations . . . ; there are here,
among 1,069 professional people, 361 teachers or proprietors of
Hebrew schools.

There are in this particular section of this city as many as
306 synagogues. There are 22 churches and a Mission House,
which are closed all the time. . . .

On May 13, 1903, there were 72 pleasure places, clubs of the
people, literary and social.

It will interest you to know that, in 306 synagogues, 276 of
them are regular, only 30 are special, not counting what is done
during the holidays. . . . The total number of seats in these 306
synagogues amounts to 71,024. Now the men mostly attend the
service and when they count seats they never take into consideration the juniors, the young men under 16, and the women,
who form a very small percentage.

. . . Only 25 were regular synagogues; the rest, while they are
regular organized places of worship, yet during the week they
are used for different purposes. Thirty-seven are used during the
week for dancing purposes; 77 are shops and factories; 36 in the
rear of saloons; 19 are halls and private places.

It may interest you to learn something about the *cheders*
[Hebrew schools]. When I speak of the *cheder,* it does not take
in the religious schools of the Alliance. With 307 *cheders,* there
are 8,616 boys and 361 girls . . . from eight years to eighteen
years.

. . . The average income of a teacher per month is $80 and
yet the total amount paid out in this neighborhood for instruc-

A Lower East Side Hebrew school(cheder). (American Jewish Archives)

tion amounts to $10,000 a month. . . . The *cheders* are not supported by outsiders but by the people of the Lower East Side.

There are four theaters in this neighborhood. One of them is open on Friday, Saturday, and Sunday, and the rest of the week it is always open for performances of the societies of the neighborhood. Each house brings in at least $1,000 and any society that wants to can hire the theater, except for such an affair. Now they have four afternoons in the week, sixteen performances a week in four theaters, given by benevolent societies, lodges, unions, synagogues, and sometimes private individuals if they need to raise money, and the others help along selling tickets, and in that way I say an average of $1,800 a week is raised from pleasure. . . . I think $1,000,000 is being raised by the people of this neighborhood to ameliorate the condition of the people who have not had the advantages of an education.

From an address quoted in *Memoirs of David Blaustein*,
by Miriam Blaustein, McBride & Nast, 1913, pp. 138–141

BORIS D. BOGEN Remembers His Pioneering in Jewish Social Work, 1904–1910

Strange as it may seem, a surplus of three hundred dollars was the seed from which sprang a most significant and extraordinary enterprise, the Federation of Jewish Philanthropies and Jewish Welfare Funds. In 1820 a poor lonely Jew, a veteran of the American Revolutionary War, drew the concern of a few Jews who then raised funds to help him financially. They named themselves the Hebrew Benevolent Society. When the veteran died, a sum of three hundred dollars was left over; this was used as seed money for the organization of the Hebrew Orphan Asylum. In 1874, the successful experience of the Hebrew Orphan Asylum stimulated the founding of the United Hebrew Charities (see Part Two, selection 27) which in turn was the forebearer of the magnificent and multifaceted New York Federation of Jewish Philanthropies. The Federation comprises Jewish institutions within the community: the Welfare Funds, in the main; the United Israel Appeal; the Joint Distribution Committee; and national organizations. In 1973 it was combined with the United Jewish Appeal.

The Federation and Welfare Funds ideas are basically an expression of the high ideal of *tzedakah* (literally, righteousness), sharing our wealth with the needy, the handicapped, the unfortunate. It has been the Jewish way of life from its very beginnings as a people. In America, *tzedakah* has flowered as in no other land. It has served as an example to American communities which have patterned their Community Chests and United Funds along Federation principles. *Tzedakah* is a potent unifying force of American

Founders of the Joint Distribution Committee. Seated in the fore-
ground (right) are Jacob H. Schiff, Arthur Lehman, Cyrus Adler;
(left) Felix Warburg, Louis Marshall; (standing, left) Herbert H.
Lehman. (Joint Distribution Committee)

Jewry. The Federation has prevented waste, rivalry, and duplication and has made possible an ongoing program of community planning, coordination, and unification. It has accustomed American Jews to giving annually to support the causes of creative Jewish survival. It encompasses the care and welfare of those at home and abroad, aiding hospitals, family welfare, Jewish education, homes for the aged, community centers, and diverse agencies. The Welfare Funds has raised hundreds of millions of dollars for relief and rehabilitation of the victims of nazism, Arab persecution, and Soviet oppression. They have helped build the State of Israel.

The Federation idea was sponsored chiefly by German Jewish immigrants, with the first two federations established in Boston (1895) and Cincinnati (1896). In the excerpt that follows, Boris D. Bogen, one of the early social workers in America, narrates his experiences as director of the Cincinnati Jewish community during its formative years (1904–1910).

"Social service was . . . the medium of religion. . . ."

I LEFT Cincinnati distressed by many doubts. If this place were offered, ought I take it? . . . I had been a teacher; this was a new profession for me. But doubt quickly changed to decision when a telegram from Cincinnati notified me that I had been chosen. I accepted. . . .

I went to New York to sit for two weeks under the tutelage of Dr. Frankel [a Jewish communal leader (1867–1931) who was interested in social service, public health, insurance, and overseas relief work], to attend meetings of his committees, to go with case workers in the field. . . .

"Do not hurry to introduce innovations or changes," he said. "Just do as your predecessor did. When you are absolutely certain that you have convinced at least a majority of your board that you measure up to their standards, then and then only begin slowly and cautiously to introduce your own ideas. I should say the first six months not a single new idea, not a single new measure, not a single change." . . .

Relief was the best part of our work in Cincinnati. We gave our afflicted bread, but our effort chiefly was to enable them to earn their bread, and so for this one we bought a horse and wagon that he might go about peddling, and for that one we established a small store.

When public health service still was in a most elementary state, we were conducting a clinic . . . and providing visiting nurses. We went into the field of education to establish a manual-training school for our boys because manual training was then lacking in the public schools. . . .

We treated tuberculosis as a social disease, providing adequate relief not only for the patient but also for his family. . . .

The patient was not compelled to separate from his family; if he was sent to a sanitorium, the family was established in the city where the sanitorium was located. If he remained in Cincinnati, a comfortable home was secured for the entire family. . . . An adequate allowance would be provided and, as soon as the patient was in condition . . . steps were taken to assist the family reestablish itself on a self-supporting basis. . . .

We experimented also with the "treatment" of deserted families, working on the assumption that Jewish family desertion has unique features. . . . When a Jew leaves his family, it is apt to be because the endless struggle to make ends meet and the miserable surroundings have become more than even loyal devotion can bear; if he leaves, the family will be looked after by charity —they will be better off without him.

So we would refuse to give aid to a deserted family, allowing the non-Jewish relief agencies to handle the case. The wandering husband was notified through the press that, unless he was heard from, the family would be broken up; the Jewish Charities would not concern itself where the father himself was indifferent. In the meantime the National Desertion Bureau would conduct the search.

In most cases the man would return quickly and anxiously; we would take up his problem with him and would try to find a way out of the material hopelessness. . . . Within a few years family desertion had decreased almost to the vanishing point.

This determination to treat the family as the unit . . . guided us in dealing with Jewish orphans. In an age of enthusiasm for bigger and better orphan asylums, we tried to place dependent children in supervised boarding homes. When one hundred and twenty-five pogrom orphans were brought to America for adoption into Jewish homes, the Cincinnati community accepted eight of them, only to discover that they were all of one family, brothers and sisters. True to Jewish tradition and Cincinnati policy, we determined to keep the entire family intact by boarding out all eight in one home. Finding the home was not, however, a simple task. Finally, my wife and I agreed to add them to our own six youngsters. . . .

. . . It was important that . . . the Jewish youth should be kept from assimilation with the cheapening influences of tenement life. We must emphasize Jewishness as something worthwhile; we must encourage activities that might strengthen the tie . . . between the old generation and the new, bridging over the widening gap between them. In the midst of plans for club activities, classes, entertainments, and lectures, I sought continually for means of emphasizing this Jewish note. Jewish movements of all kinds were encouraged to make the Settlement their center. Jewish holidays were celebrated by community gatherings and festivities; at the *seder* table in the Settlement auditorium, families reserved places year after year and the neighborhood girls joined hands with the women of our board in serving the guests; at Purim the children's clubs conducted a public presentation of gifts to parents.

One year we staged a "Jews of Many Lands Exposition." The entire building was utilized for booths, each one representing the settlement of Jews in another land, and each presided over by men and women in the picturesque costume of that land.

It was the pride of this Cincinnati Jewry to be known as the exemplar of social service . . . and everywhere Jewish charities were being federated as ours was.

Social service was . . . the medium of religion in the Reform Jewry of Cincinnati; it was religion. In the Hebrew Union College there was established a social-service course for the embryonic rabbis and I was the teacher. This was a new thing in theological seminaries. . . .

That the devoted hands of Jewry would have enough work to do for many, many years to come in serving the immigrant was never questioned. . . . The Russian pogroms were driving our brethren to us in vast numbers and our favorite altars were at their feet; and we made no end of serving them.

We had no international problems of Jewry on our hands, save . . . the passport matter in Russia. Jews of whatever nationality were not admitted to Russia though they carried the passports of their governments. This, however, was an academic issue since so few Jews sought the pleasure of touring in Russia. . . .

. . . We were not then burdened with the worry of perpetuating Judaism in America, nor did we hear much of Jewish education. We knew that, as long as these Jews from Europe came to us, Jewish life would not only be perpetuated but also enriched. . . .

From *Born a Jew,* by Boris D. Bogen and Alfred Segal,
MacMillan and Co., 1930, pp. 76–81

AN ALUMNUS Describes the Students' Strike at Yeshiva Rabbi Itzhak Elhanan, 1908

Talmud Torah, the "study of *Torah*" (in its broadest sense), has been a paramount lifelong duty of Jews. It is prescribed in the Holy Scriptures (*Deuteronomy* 6:4-9) and reiterated in *Pirke Avot* (*Ethics of the Fathers*) which contains a distillation of the teachings of the sages. Jews may not use their knowledge of *Torah* to their own personal advantage. They must be ever diligent and alert in pursuing study for its own sake, neither for gain nor glory nor as a "tool" for earning a livelihood.

In the New World, Orthodox Jews implanted the ancient ideal of *talmud Torah* through *yeshivot* (*Torah* academies). They defined *Torah* almost exclusively as the study of *Talmud* and its commentaries.

The first *yeshivah* in America was founded on the Lower East Side by Russian and Polish Jews on September 15, 1886. Named Etz Chayim (Tree of Life), a term used to describe the *Torah,* it was intended for boys of elementary and high school age. Secular studies, as well as the Hebrew and Yiddish languages, were taught casually after 4:00 P.M. A year later Yeshiva Rabbi Itzhak Elhanan was established for older students; it was incorporated in 1897.

For a decade the Yeshiva underwent the pangs of "Americanization." The founders were motivated by Old World principles and standards. It was not viewed as a professional school to prepare rabbis for the burgeoning Jewish communities. There was no fixed course of study, no set program requiring years of attendance, no final examinations or diplomas. As in the Old Country, a candidate who wanted to be ordained had to appear before one or more recognized talmudic scholars to receive *semichah* (a document attesting to his learning and authority to function as a rabbi). Secular studies were alien. Students who enrolled in evening schools to learn English speech and literature were looked upon with disfavor. Also unwelcome were courses in Hebrew, history, homiletics (the art of preaching), and *Chochmat Yisrael* (the Science of Judaism) which were taught in the Conservative Jewish Theological Seminary, New York, and the Reform Hebrew Union College, Cincinnati, Ohio.

Yeshiva University, as we know it today, with its graduate schools in medicine, social work, Hebrew religious education, and law, in addition to its rabbinical school, evolved because the students insisted on an institution that would meet the needs of American Jewry. They reorganized the situation in the new land and they fought it out with an American technique—a strike. A description of that students' strike follows.

". . . The students are employees of the Board of Trustees and have no right to interfere in the policies established by them."

IN 1896, the venerated and beloved spiritual head of Orthodox Jewry, Rabbi Itzhak Elhanan Spektor of Kovno, died. Two of his disciples in New York, whom he had ordained as rabbis, felt it their moral duty to perpetuate his memory. One, Rabbi Meyer Matlin, proposed to his colleague, Rabbi Judah Bernstein [Rabbi Moses Meyer Matlin came to America in 1890 and was the supervisor of the ritual slaughterers under Rabbi Jacob Joseph (see selection 5) and also of the *kashrut* of the products of the California Wine Association. He was a reputed scholar and a saintly person. The author of this memoir came to know Rabbi Matlin well in Sioux City, Iowa, where they were neighbors.

The original main building, Yeshiva University. (Yeshiva University)

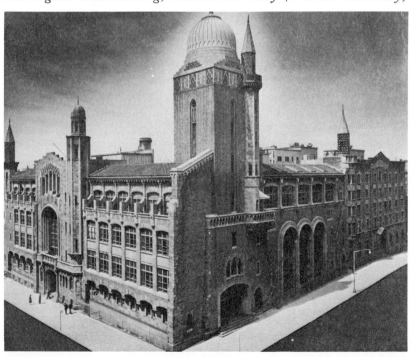

Rabbi Yehuda David Bernstein was a child prodigy in *Talmud* and mathematics and an authority on Maimonides. Known for his deep piety, he, too, became a supervisor in a wine distillery on the East Side where he eked out a modest living.], that the most appropriate memorial would be to establish a talmudical seminary in the name of their teacher. There was no scarcity of prospective students for Jewish immigration in 1897 was high. Among the newcomers were many talmudical students from famous higher schools of learning in Lithuania.

Qualified youths were invited to Rabbi Matlin's home and the project was started. Each was promised a stipend of $2 per week to meet living expenses. Rabbi Matlin taught without salary. The school met at his home rent free. No other costs were involved so that the total budget was $25 a week. Elderly Jews were engaged to solicit contributions at a salary of 45 per cent of their collections. Rabbi Bernstein, the fiscal administrator, was also a volunteer. The school was set up and [it] prospered.

The number of students grew, and in 1906 the Yeshiva moved to a synagogue on Forsythe Street. It soon became necessary to buy a building to accommodate the student body. With an initial gift of $1,000 from the great philanthropist Jacob Schiff, the Yeshiva acquired an old building at 156 Henry Street. In 1908 the enrollment reached one hundred. The weekly stipend was raised from $2.50 to $4.00. [A student who received $2.75 weekly recalled his budgeting as follows: 75 cents weekly for lodging, 25 cents daily for food, and the remaining 25 cents for all the other needs of the week, mostly medicine to supplement the lack of proper nourishment, relates Gilbert Klaperman in *The Story of Yeshiva University*, Macmillan, 1969, p. 96.] The program was extended; a secretary and a *shamas* [ritual assistant] were added to the staff. A supervising rabbi was engaged . . . Rabbi Nahum Baron who would walk through the classes making sure that the students concentrated on their studies and helping them when he was needed. He was dubbed the "walking delegate."

The economic panic of 1907, when real estate values plunged drastically, caused a shrinkage in funds. To meet the pressing

financial needs, collectors were engaged to solicit in the North-
east, Midwest, and Canadian Jewish communities. They were
paid 50 per cent of their collections plus travel expenses. Students were also enlisted to preach and make appeals in synagogues. The expenses had mounted considerably. In addition to
the large student body, there were office costs for a secretary, a
janitor, a *shamas*, light, and fuel. As a result, the weekly payments
to the students were often delayed. A week or two might pass
without the students receiving their stipends. In 1908, the situation became critical; a few weeks had already passed, and the
students had not received money to live on.

During the eleven years of its existence, there had been no
graduation from the Yeshiva. Those who were fortunate to find
grace in the eyes of the Board of Trustees were selected as
grooms for their daughters. When Rabbi Bernstein was once
asked how long the Yeshiva would last, he cynically replied, "As
long as there will be 'ugly ducklings' among Jews."

In 1908, learning about a number of strikes in New York City,
such as the bakers' strike, teamsters' strike, needleworkers' strike,
and others, some of the students had a brilliant idea that they
too would strike. However, they felt that, in order to gain the
sympathy of the public, the strike must be based not on economic
but on educational and moral grounds. They formulated a series
of demands requiring that a fixed number of years for study be
determined for graduation and ordination as rabbi. They asked
that, in addition to *Talmud*, they be required to study the Bible,
the art of preaching, and English literature. The student body
selected a committee of three to present their claims to the
Board of Directors.

The chairman of the Board of Trustees was Nehemiah Lamport, a prosperous merchant. When the committee of three presented their demands with the ultimatum to strike, Mr. Lamport
replied: "I never permit my employees to discuss the policy of
my business. The students are employees of the Board of Trustees and have no right to interfere in the policies established by
them. The very fact that they threaten a strike indicates that

they have already been poisoned by the virus of socialism. I therefore recommend that the three students be dismissed immediately so the others would take heed and act more obediently."
When the committee reported Mr. Lamport's remarks to the
students, they decided to strike. On April 26, 1908, the strike
began. [For a detailed account of the strike, read chapter 6 of
Klaperman's book on Yeshiva University, mentioned earlier in this
selection.]

On that very date I came to enroll in the Yeshiva carrying
with me a letter of recommendation from Rabbi B. L. Levinthal,
Chief Rabbi of Philadelphia, who was also a Trustee of the
Yeshiva. When my father . . . and I approached 156 Henry
Street, we were astonished to find groups of students outside,
gesticulating and arguing heatedly. At the door stood two students with clubs in their hands guarding the entrance. Inno-
cently, I said that I had come to study.

"We are on a strike today," replied the students.

"What is a strike?" I asked.

"A strike means students don't study."

"And what if one wants to study?"

"Then he is a scab."

"What is a scab?" I asked.

"A strike-breaker, and his bones will be broken!"

Father understood the danger, and we withdrew.

Ultimately Mr. Lamport resigned, and Mr. Sam Willner succeeded him as Chairman of the Board. He promised that the
three students of the committee would be reinstated and that
payments would be made regularly. Also that a committee would
be appointed to study the other issues raised, and that a course
in English literature would be instituted immediately. Unfortunately, they selected a former student of the Yeshiva to teach
English. He had no knowledge of pedagogy. He brought with
him Dickens's *David Copperfield,* and he would read a line and
translate it into Yiddish. Some of the hundred students in the
course didn't know one word of English while others had an ele-

mentary school training. The number of students dwindled from week to week, and the instructor was left all alone. Thus the Yeshiva English course came to an end.

In August of 1908, the situation worsened again. Payments of weekly stipends were skipped, the students became embittered, and a new strike (which proved to be the last one) was declared. The Board of Trustees met and declared the Yeshiva closed and all students were dismissed. Students had no claim on the Yeshiva whatsoever. Rabbi Masliansky and Rabbi Jaffee sided with the students, but their influence did not go far.

The students opened a *yeshiva* of their own, calling it Yeshivat Ha-Rabbanim, "Yeshiva for Rabbis." They found quarters on East Broadway, for which they didn't have to pay rent. They sent out collectors throughout the land but could not compete with the experienced collectors of the old Yeshiva. After a desperate struggle of three months, a goodly number of the students left the *yeshiva* and became rabbis or Hebrew school teachers, while some entered business and some found brides.

Finally the Board of Trustees reopened the Yeshiva which was located at 156 Henry Street near the Etz Chaim Yeshiva, and every student had to pass a personality test and promise never to go on strike. A new cadre of students formed the nucleus of the new *yeshiva*. About one-half of the former students were readmitted after having passed the "personality test."

In 1906 a young man, Bernard (Dov) Revel, who was endowed with great gifts of scholarship, piety, vision, and leadership, came to America from Lithuania and studied at the Yeshiva for a brief period. He soon enrolled at New York University where he received his master's degree and went on to complete his doctorate at Dropsie College for Jewish Studies where he received the first Ph.D. degree in 1912. His reputation as a scholar in *Talmud*, general knowledge, and science brought him to the attention of the distinguished Rabbinical Board of the Yeshiva. In 1915 he was elected to head the secular and regular departments of the Yeshiva. He organized a faculty of scholars who had made their reputations as teachers of *Talmud* and Codes, *Chochmat Yisrael* (the Science of Judaism), American History, Bible, Pedagogy, Hebrew Biblical and Aramaic Grammar, Homiletics (preaching). He served as the head of the institution for twenty-five years until his death in 1940. It was he who laid the foundation which was built up into the expanded world-renowned institution by the late Dr. Samuel Belkin.

From a personal memoir,
written at the invitation of the editor,
by Rabbi Hayim Reuven Rabinowitz, Jerusalem

DR. GEORGE J. GORDON
Describes the Development of the
Minneapolis Talmud Torah, 1911

Many immigrants, especially unattached young men, left turbulent New York and pushed westward. In 1894, eighteen-year-old George J. Gordon wound up in Minneapolis where he found nearly 6,000 Jews, several synagogues and charitable organizations, as well as a Hebrew Free School. In Lithuania, he had studied at the noted *yeshivah* in Tels and he found the Minneapolis Hebrew schools sadly lacking. He was determined to do something about it, but he knew that other things had to come first. He enrolled in the public high school and then went on to a medical school where he earned his M.D. He settled on the North Side, the prime Jewish neighborhood at that time, where he acquired a fine reputation and a large clientele. Later he became a faculty member in a medical college in the Twin Cities, Minneapolis and St. Paul.

As he grew in his profession, Gordon devoted himself to the cause of Hebrew education. His "baby" was the Minneapolis Talmud Torah. In time, many of the babies he brought into the world became supporters of the school. He implanted, in the East European Jewish community, a spirit of self-worth and pride and, in German Jewish families, a feeling of kinship with their immigrant brothers and sisters. When he retired from his medical practice, he dedicated his full-time efforts to the school and its many activities.

For decades the Minneapolis Talmud Torah has been a leader and model for communal Hebrew education on this continent. Its generations of graduates have enriched Jewish life in America and in Israel, thanks to the vision and devotion of an inspired man.

In the excerpt which follows, George J. Gordon (no
relation to the author of the book from which this
selection is excerpted) describes the beginnings of
the school.

". . . If you wanted a good school you had to pay good salaries to good teachers. . . ."

I WAS GOING to North Side High School in 1894. I was then
twenty years old, and I was doing my best to make up for the
secular training I had missed in Europe. I could not forget how
much Hebrew education had done for me, and I felt . . . that the
cheder [Hebrew school] system here, with its very poor teachers
and no method worthy of the name and poor classrooms and un-
graded classes, was certainly not the kind of school that ought to
be developed in an American Jewish community. I couldn't see
how very much knowledge could be acquired under these circumstances. . . . So I called together a number of people and we
held a series of meetings to decide on what we wanted to teach
our children.

. . . We had a pretty fair idea of what we really wanted to include in our curriculum. We not only wanted our children to
know their Bible and history but we wanted them to know the
Hebrew language, . . . to speak it naturally. But of course the
times weren't really right for the kind of advanced school that
I wanted. All we could do then was to secure a room over on
Fifth Street North, and we brought a Hebrew teacher from
Fargo, North Dakota. We paid him forty dollars a month. He
really wasn't too good, but he was certainly better than what
we had had. . . .

In 1898 we decided to transfer the school to the Kenesseth
Israel Synagogue. We secured a new teacher and with the help
of the synagogue officials . . . built a four-room building in the
back of the synagogue. Then we set ourselves the task of secur-
ing some really good teachers, and we began to have some ex-

cellent results. Our classes met from four to eight o'clock in the evening every day in the week. We had about 75 pupils. . . . Still the school was not too good.

There were too many people who were opposing the kind of ideas I had, and the program was still not good enough. I organized a revolt against the old *Talmud Torah* and all its inadequacies. One of the teachers had asked for an increase in salary and because of this his contract was not renewed. I felt people had to understand that if you wanted a good school you had to pay good salaries to good teachers . . . , so I just urged everybody whom I knew to refrain from helping the old school. That was how we really got started. The old school simply couldn't keep going without our support.

In 1910 I got together a group of men on the North Side who were themselves learned Jews. They were convinced that the old *cheder* of East European origin could not thrive on American soil. We realized how important it was to teach our Jewish youths in accordance with modern methods, and we realized the necessity of integrating Jewish life into American life. We did not want our children to make unfavorable comparisons between the Hebrew school and the public school.

In February 1911, our new school, consisting of four classrooms, was opened. It was a vast improvement over anything that had ever been offered to Jewish parents and children. We had an enrollment of approximately 115 children. . . . A group of men personally solicited funds from members of the community in order to keep it going. The school grew. In 1913 there were 264 students enrolled. Then we changed the name of the school to the Talmud Torah of Minneapolis. By 1914 the school population had grown so that our building became overcrowded.

On April 17, 1915, we dedicated our new building, which had cost $45,000, and on the same day we graduated our first class of seventeen boys and three girls. Shortly after, an alumni association was formed, and it has grown so that there are now over 800 members. Many of the graduates have become rabbis. Others are active in Jewish community life, here and throughout the country, and we are very proud of them. In 1916 we organized a high school department, and we graduated six students in that first high school graduation. We also, in 1920, established a college course of study which we called the *beth hamidrash* (house of study). In order to graduate [from] all the departments a child has to attend our school for ten years.

We were one of the first institutions in the country to teach Hebrew by using it as the language of conversation in the classrooms. All our classes and all our subjects were taught in Hebrew. Our school reached its highest development in 1930 when we had a total enrollment of 800. Thirty-six per cent of the pupils enrolled in 1943 actually graduated, as against the national record of Hebrew schools of only 5 per cent.

From *Jews in Transition,* by Albert I. Gordon, 1949, pp. 179–181. Reprinted by permission of the publisher, the University of Minnesota Press

MORRIS ROSENFELD Reports about the Triangle Fire That Shocked America into Action, 1911

On the Saturday afternoon of March 25, 1911, New York's famous Washington Square was the scene of a disaster which still reverberates in American history—the Triangle (Shirtwaist Company) fire. (A comprehensive account of this catastrophe in vivid, dramatic detail is the subject of a book entitled *The Triangle Fire*, by Louis Stein [J.B. Lippincott, 1962], illustrated with documentary photographs and striking cartoons which had appeared, at that time, in the New York press.)

In the fire, 146 employees of the Triangle Shirtwaist Company, mostly women, were burned or crushed, choked or jumped to their deaths. The bodies of seven victims were buried unidentified.

The city was convulsed with grief, hysteria, and feelings of public guilt. The press cried out in outrage; the protest meetings, the services in various houses of prayer, the demonstrations, the memorial meetings—all drew hundreds of thousands of guilt-ridden citizens. The public conscience was deeply stirred. Hearings and trials were instituted; 723 arrests were made.

The Triangle fire brought home the misery of working conditions in the shops and led to the overthrow of the wretched "system." Powerful labor unions arose to demand and force decent standards and working conditions from the manufacturers. Among the leaders were the Jewish unions like the International Ladies Garment Workers Union (ILGWU).

The news report that follows was written by Morris Rosenfeld (1862-1923), a reporter for the *Jewish Daily Forward,* who had worked in a sweatshop when he came to New York in 1886. His Yiddish poems de-

Dear Mr. Editer.

i went down town with my daddy
yesterday to see that terrible fire
where all the littel girls jumped out
of high windows My littel cousin Beatrice
and i are sending you five dollars a
piece from our savings bank to help
them out of trubble please give it to

the right one to use it for ~~————~~
sombody whose littel girl jumped out
of a window i wouldent like to jump
out of a high window myself.

Yours Truly
Morris Butler

Letter sent with a contribution to help families of the victims of the Triangle Shirtwaist Company fire. (Signature of 450,000, a publication on the occasion of the 65th Anniversary Convention of the International Ladies' Garment Workers' Union, May 1965) scribing the life of the immigrant became very popular and came to the attention of Professor Leo Wiener of Harvard. Professor Wiener translated them into an English volume, *Songs of the Ghetto,* which won acclaim in the United States and Europe. His poems were translated into many European tongues as well as into Japanese and Hebrew.

"The sidewalks were littered with the dead and wounded."

THE FIRE broke out mid-afternoon. The building (located on Washington Place [at the] corner [of] Greene Street) is ten-floors high. The top three were occupied by the Triangle Waist Company, and this is where the fire started.

The flames spread quickly. A stream of fire tore through the elevators and the stairs to the upper floors. Instantaneously the fire was visible through all the windows, as tongues of flame climbed higher and higher, enveloping the helpless victims.

The veritable whirlpool of fire swept the floors, growing, terrifying, killing. The workers on the top floors could not endure the heat and smoke. One after another they began to jump down [from the window ledges] on the eighth, ninth, and tenth floors and plunged dead, their clothes burning, on the sidewalks. When the corpses began to pile up (about thirty bodies) the fire engines began to arrive. The firemen were powerless. [The nets that were spread to catch them were torn from the grasp of firemen who held them or were ripped open because of the weight of the falling bodies.] The fire ladders reached the seventh floor. They stood helpless and looked on as one after another plunged to the street like dead birds. . . . Men held out longer but when they could not endure the inferno they, too, jumped. . . .

Below, thousands of workers from neighboring factories and bystanders watched horrified; their sobbing and wailing rent the air. Horrifying, unforgettable scenes flash in rapid succession. On the eighth floor a young couple appears at the window. He holds her fast. Behind them flames ignite their clothes. He embraces her tenderly, kisses her gently, and releases her. She jumps and hits the sidewalk. In the next moment he follows her, his body striking hard by her corpse. Both are dead. Above, a sea of fire surged in great waves and clouds of smoke billowed and enveloped the top floors. Now and then the smoke clouds are blown aside, exposing burned, twisted bodies. The flames enshroud the stairs and fill the elevator shafts. An elevator catches fire and comes crashing down. Three others are still working and have succeeded in rescuing about a hundred girls. The elevator men fear to risk a third trip. Hundreds of girls left stranded at the top cry hysterically; their cries rend the heart as the flames lick closer. Desperately they stampede to the roof, the fire escapes, and to the open windows. . . .

Suddenly a fearful crash is heard. The seventh floor has collapsed. Scores of girls, who were crowded near the elevator shaft, are hurled into a sea of flames. Later their bodies were found lying one on top of the other.

It took a full hour before the firemen could penetrate into the burning factory; by that time it was all over. The sidewalks were littered with the dead and wounded. No longer was there anyone visible at the windows. Those who were doomed in the building were lying somewhere burned or asphyxiated from the smoke. [There was a rickety fire escape consisting of a ladder leading to a small rear courtyard. A narrow door led to it. Workers jammed to flee the inferno and many lost their lives in the attempt.]

There were not sufficient ambulances and patrol wagons available to remove the wounded and the dead. Surrounding stores were transformed into emergency wards and morgues. Grocers, butchers, and peddlers loaned their delivery vehicles and pushcarts to cart the dead to the morgue.

Ten minutes ago, before I began to write this, a door flew open and a young man burst in weeping hysterically, his hands motioning wildly, his face wet with tears.

"I was there. I saw it," he muttered and was struck dumb. A

little later he sobbed out the dreadful story. Every time he recalled the tragic incidents, he moaned. . . .

Translated from the Yiddish by the editor

From *Bletter fun Mein Leben* (*Pages from My Life*), Vol. V,
by Abraham Cahan, Forvertz Association, 1926–1931, pp. 12–15

[Postscript:]

For long weeks, *The Forward* carried stories, banners, lines such as: "Funerals Replace Weddings . . ."; "Unparalleled Tragedies: 29 Bodies Unidentified . . ."; "A Closet of Wedding Clothes —All That Is Left of Yetta Shapiro . . ."; "The Only Remains, a Silent Violin . . ."; "Mother Incinerated, Son Asphyxiated, Three Orphans Living . . ."; and, under a recent wedding photograph— "Becky Kesler, the Bride, Burned to Death. . . ."

A YOUNG GIRL Attends
the Yiddish Theater, about 1911

The Yiddish theater was born in Rumania over a hundred years ago; its centennial was celebrated by Rumanian Jews in September, 1976. Acting had been frowned upon in the Old Country because it was considered frivolous and unworthy of the sedate folk of the *shtetl* except on Purim when such restraints were relaxed. Amateur *Purimspieler* (players) and minstrels improvised amusing merrymaking.

The Yiddish theater took hold and developed on the Lower East Side in the 1880s, filling an urgent social need in the Jewish community. Going to the theater was a gala family event, an escape from the sweatshops and the drab tenements. It brought back nostalgic memories of the "other side." Benefit performances were occasions for the *landsleit* (hometowners) societies to get together and renew old friendships.

The Yiddish actors were adored and imitated by old and young alike. Plays ran about a month each; performances were long and encores many. The rapport between the actors and the audience was manifest throughout. The audience got its money's worth. People returned as often as they could save up the admission cost which started at 25 cents.

The following selection reflects a young girl's excitement at attending the Yiddish theater. Its author, Sophie Ruskay, was born on the East Side in the days of horsecars and cobblestone streets. Her book, *Horsecars and Cobblestones,* affords an authentic picture of the life of a middleclass American Jewish family at the turn of this century.

Above: Grand Street Theater, Lower East Side; its marquee featuring the great Yiddish actor, Jacob Adler. (American Jewish Archives)
Below: Stars of the Yiddish theater in the 1890s. (Right to left) Jacob Adler, Sigmund Feinman, Sigmund Mogulesco, Rudolph Marx, Max Abramovitch, and David Kessler. (Yivo-Yiddish Scientific Institute)

"To me, all plays were good, even the bad ones."

THE YIDDISH THEATER on the East Side was flourishing. Great actors from Europe were glad to perform before such an admiring and appreciative audience. Like the Synagogue and the Annual Ball, the theater served as a social function. There was no reserve among the audience; everyone talked to everyone else. During the intermission it was a common sight to see some well-cushioned ladies standing in the orchestra aisle waving their arms or making sounds like "pst, pst" to attract the attention of friends in the gallery and converse across the vast expanse of the theater. "How's Mama's feet?" or "Did you hear who died last week?" There would be voluble "tut-tuts" and sympathetic wagging of heads. Those who were near listened with undisguised interest, except when too busy talking themselves. Others sociably and noisily drank soda water purchased from the ushers who marched up and down the aisles, shrilly calling, "Candy, soda water, candy, soda water!"

Some of the plays were classics, such as *The Kreutzer Sonata; Gott, Mensh, und Teufel* [*God, Man, and Devil*]; and works by Shakespeare. I remember a Shylock played by the great tragedian Jacob Adler who gave me an unforgettable memory of that great role. Some years later, Adler played it on Broadway, in Yiddish, with an entire English-speaking cast. . . . There were still others like Madame [Bertha] Kalish who . . . became an English-speaking star. . . . Although enormously successful on her tour through the states, she came back time and again to the East Side, playing again before her *Yiddishe volk* [Jewish people]. . . .

But it was the simple drama of our own day which I preferred. To me, all plays were good, even the bad ones. Not understanding Yiddish too well . . . I relied almost entirely upon the acting which was so natural and expressive. . . .

There was one play which served as a pattern for many others. It was the story of a family that had come to America. The son, after a few years, had grown prosperous. He had discarded his religious practices as old-fashioned and was embarrassed when his aged parents visited his now ultrafashionable home. He felt he did his duty by providing for their material needs, but this, the father told him, had now become "gall and wormwood in their mouths."

In a scene bordering on the tragic, the mother, in ritual wig [the *sheitel*], dressed in Old-World grandeur, tries in vain to ingratiate herself with her American-born daughter-in-law and her grandchildren. They look upon her as someone strange and alien. The father succeeds no better. He reminds his son, "Your Milton is past eleven . . . time he was learning for *Bar Mitzvah*."

"Please, father, spare me that," says the son as he looks uncomfortably at his friends who are at a table playing pinochle and are highly amused by such a suggestion.

Brokenhearted, the father dies. The grave yawns right before the audience; nothing is left to the imagination.

"I repent, I repent!" says the son as he tries to fling himself into the grave.

The aged mother restrains him, and there follows a tearful reconciliation. "You can perform a *mitzvah* [good deed] that will bring joy to your father in Paradise," she says. "Your great-uncle's only child is an old maid; already she is twenty. If you, my son, will provide the wedding and the dowry for this penniless orphan, a husband can be found."

With the assistance of the *shadchan* [marriage broker], a comic but nostalgic figure to those who so recently came from Europe but an object of ridicule to the American-born children, the match is made. The *chupah* [wedding canopy] is brought on the stage and, after a ceremony in which tears flow freely, there are feasting and rejoicing. The *shamas* [sexton], his red bandana streaming from his coattails, starts a traditional dance in a circle; all clap hands as they beat out the rhythm. . . . The curtain falls.

To Mama and to us it was all simply wonderful.

From *Horsecars and Cobblestones*, by Sophie Ruskay, Beechhurst Press, 1948, pp. 50–54. Reprinted by permission of A. S. Barnes and Company, Inc.

LOTTA LEVENSOHN Recounts the Beginnings of Hadassah, 1912

When Henrietta Szold and her mother visited Palestine in November of 1909, they were appalled at the disease, poverty, filth, and starvation which they saw. Mrs. Szold told her daughter, "Here is work for you. This is what your group ought to be doing."

There was so very much to be done by Henrietta Szold's little Zionist circle. It went to work and, in so doing, grew into the great national organization of Hadassah, the healer and guardian of the health of *Eretz Yisrael*. Hadassah maintains hospitals and clinics, nursing services and infant welfare, milk stations and school lunch programs, day care centers and playgrounds. Every chapter in Marlin Levin's *Balm of Gilead: The Story of Hadassah* reads like a "thriller."

While supported by Jewish women, Hadassah's facilities never turn away Arabs, Christians, or anyone who comes to them for aid. And, as soon as Israeli agencies are able to take over, Hadassah turns over its projects to them.

Hadassah's great hour came during World War II when it saved almost 150,000 Jewish youths doomed to destruction in Nazi Europe (and, after 1948, in hostile Moslem countries). At the age of 75, Miss Szold heroically conceived of the Youth Aliyah program and went to work again.

In Jerusalem, Hadassah, simultaneously with the Hebrew University, built two great medical centers, including a medical school, which are the finest in the Middle East and are world renowned.

Today Hadassah embraces a membership of over 300,000, making it the largest women's Zionist organization in the world.

Lotta Levensohn was secretary to Dr. Judah Leon

First American nurses arrive in Eretz Yisrael, 1913, courtesy of Hadassah. (Hadassah)

Magnes when Dr. Magnes was honorary secretary of
the Federation of American Zionists. In the following
selection she retraces some of the early steps in the
history of Hadassah.

". . . Wherever Miss Szold sat . . . , there was the head of the table."

THE IDEA of a woman's Zionist study group emerged in 1906
or early in 1907 from a discussion between Dr. Judah Leon
Magnes, then honorary secretary of the Federation of American
Zionists, and myself as his secretary.

A few women's Zionist societies did already exist here and
there. However, many, if not most, of their members had only
vague, romantic ideas about Zionism. . . . Lacking a coherent
programme of Zionist education and what Henrietta Szold was
later to call "a specific project in Palestine," the members sooner
or later lost interest and drifted away.

Dr. Magnes asked if I could suggest ways and means of re-
cruiting women for the Zionist organization and keeping them
interested. I replied that the first, basic step must be education
in Zionism: its aims and activities both in the Diaspora and in
Palestine. He asked me to draw up a memorandum on the subject. . . .

Dr. Magnes approved the programme and instructed me to organize a study group along the lines I had suggested. I then
called a meeting of about 20 or 25 of my Zionist girl friends
and some of their friends, . . . and the group was organized.

. . . Dr. Magnes took my breath away by suggesting that I invite Miss Henrietta Szold to join us. I was so dumbfounded at
the idea of asking so renowned a scholar and editor to study
Zionism with young girls far inferior to her in knowledge of
Zionism (or, indeed, of Judaism) that I found no words to reply. Sensing my embarrassment, Dr. Magnes kindly asked,
"Would you like *me* to invite her?" "Oh," I gasped, "if you only

would!" Thereupon he dictated a brief note circumspectly inviting her to join us as an honorary member. Within a day or two he received a characteristic note saying that she would be happy to join the Zionist study group, not, however, as an honorary but as a working member. . . . (Busy as she was with her professional and other duties, she welcomed an opportunity to teach Zionism.)

Miss Szold refused to be president of the study group and proposed Florence Robison instead. However, wherever Miss Szold sat and led the discussion, there was the head of the table.

The programme of the study group was pretty much as I had originally outlined it. The classics read and discussed included *Rome and Jerusalem* by Moses Hess; *Auto-Emancipation* by Leo Pinsker; *Pinsker and His Brochure* by Ahad Ha-Am; and *The Jewish State* by Theodor Herzl. (I must confess that we never did finish them all but we did get a fair grounding in Zionism.) There were reports on the few Zionist activities in Palestine: a few parcels of land bought by the Jewish National Fund; the commercial activities of the Anglo-Palestine Company (the Zionist bank now known as the Bank Leumi le-Israel [the National Bank of Israel]); and the struggles of the little colonies to gain a foothold. . . . Jewish topics of the day were regularly presented by Mrs. Magnes who accordingly dubbed herself the "Current Topper."

In 1909, about a year and a half after our group was organized, Miss Szold, accompanied by her mother, made her first trip to Palestine. Some of her friends confidently predicted that contact with the real Palestine would impel her to discard her Zionism. Actually . . . her Zionism had been strengthened all the more when she saw what could and should be done.

During her five weeks in Palestine, Miss Szold had been horrified to see Jewish women confined [giving birth] on the floors of their hovels in the Old City of Jerusalem with only old newspapers to wrap their newborn infants in. On her visits to schools and *Talmud Torahs* she found in some an incidence of as high as 80 per cent of trachoma among the pupils. It was then that Miss Szold's mother turned to her exclaiming, "Henrietta! It's time your girls (meaning our study group) stopped talking and did something!"

The "something" Miss Szold presented to us on her return was a plan for district visiting nursing patterned after Lillian Wald's project on the East Side of New York [see selection 9]. For support of so ambitious a project she turned at first to our group as the nucleus, but also to other groups and individuals. It was only after nearly two years of planning and preparation that a meeting was called on February 24, 1912, in the vestry rooms of Temple Emanu-El of New York for the formation of a country-wide women's Zionist organization with the twin purposes of Zionist education in America and a specific health project in Palestine. . . . The organization was first called the Daughters of Zion, while the first chapter, which was organized in New York, took the name of Hadassah in honor of Queen Esther because it was founded during the week of Purim . . . probably also because our *study group* was called Hadassah. [It is believed that, at the Rochester, New York, convention in 1914 or 1915, the name was changed, at Dr. Magnes's suggestion, to the Hadassah Women's Zionist Organization of America.]

From a Hadassah news release,
by Lotta Levensohn, January, 1967

HERBERT BAYARD SWOPE
Reports a Gangland Killing with a Far-Reaching Effect, 1912

The poverty and squalor of the ghetto took its toll. Some things new to Diaspora Jewry developed—crime and vice.

Jews had always been proud of their freedom from serious crime—thanks to a strong family life, religious devotion, and community discipline. However, the Jewish community was shocked by an article in the *North American Review* of September, 1908, by Police Commissioner Theodore Bingham, charging Jews with 50 per cent of New York's crime. The selection which follows, written by a master reporter, depicts a lurid incident in the crime picture in 1912.

Outrage at Bingham's unproven accusation was followed by an effort to bring order and self-discipline into the Jewish community. Led by the brilliant young Judah L. Magnes, then assistant rabbi of prestigious Temple Emanu-El, New York Jews tried to form a *kehilah* (community) along the lines that existed in certain European countries.

In the fall and winter of 1908-09, preliminary steps were taken. On February 27, 1909, 300 delegates representing 222 organizations convened. The meeting was chaired by Dr. Judah L. Magnes.

After some twelve years the effort fell apart, as a result of conflicting ideologies (socialism, Zionism, Orthodoxy, Reform), the paternalism of the "uptowners" toward the "downtowners," and the jumble of little synagogues, Hebrew schools, and hometown societies of *landsleit*. The ravages of World War I deflected funds into European Jewish relief and Dr. Magnes himself was diverted by his espousal of pacifism during World War I.

The failure was prophetic: later national efforts at organizing Jewry along such lines also failed. (During the Nazi era, American Jewry was unable to marshal itself to speak with one voice to President Franklin D. Roosevelt for the rescue of European Jewry.)

However, there was one lasting outcome of the *kehilah*—consolidation of educational efforts into one central Jewish education agency, now the Board of Jewish Education of New York. It became a model for similar bureaus throughout the country.

"Rosenthal had squealed once too often."

"HERMAN ROSENTHAL has squealed again."

Through the pallid underworld the sibilant whisper ran. It was heard in East Side dens; it rang in opium houses in Chinatown; it crept up to the . . . crap games of Fourteenth Street; and it reached into the more select circles of uptown gambling where business is always good and graft is always high.

Rosenthal had squealed once too often.

This time his action was a direct affront to the "'System." . . . He had publicly thrown down the gauntlet, and it was snatched up, to be returned in the form of four bullets crashing into his head while he stood in the heart of the city under a blaze of lights that enabled bystanders to follow every move of the four assassins. [They] . . . fled, secure, as they thought, from successful pursuit because they were acting under the sheltering hand of Police Lieutenant Charles Becker who had issued the order to Jack Rose:

"I want Herman Rosenthal croaked!'

But in his death Herman Rosenthal found a thousand tongues where he had been but one. His murder cried in accusation a thousandfold stronger than any he could have made . . . and now the people of the state of New York demand that two lives shall pay forfeit for every bullet fired at the man who was not permitted to tell his story.

Rosenthal squeals; Becker, the police blackmailer, and Rose, his creature, enter upon the stage. . . . And behind this trio hangs . . . the "System," in whose labyrinthian maze men are killed, others are robbed, and women are made slaves. . . .

Becker was of the "System," by the "System," and for the "System." . . . Like Caesar, all things were rendered unto Becker in the underworld. . . . Nothing escaped him. Like Briareus [in mythology, the one hundred-armed son of Uranus and Gaea and the most noted of the Uranids] he had a hundred arms. . . .

It was not a common type of man who could attain this position of power in the [New York City] Police Department. . . . He is big in girth and stature. He stands five feet eleven and weighs 190 pounds. . . . He is dark in hair and skin. His nose is straight and big . . . a mouth like the cut of a knife, and a chin that sticks out squarely at the end of a jaw like a granite block.

He is forty-two years old. He was born in Callicoon, New York . . . joined the police force in 1893. . . .

The "System" is many-sided. It can be gently kind as well as fiercely protective. It takes care of its own, and its own takes care of it. . . .

Becker began to be talked about as a coming man in police circles.

On June 22, 1911, Charles Becker, who had been made a lieutenant four years before, was detailed to the command of Special Squad No. 1, known as the "Strong-Arm Squad." From then on his history is written in blackmail and murder, in money and blood.

In ten months following his elevation to the most conspicuous position in the New York Police Department, Becker, receiving a salary of $2,250 and supporting himself and his wife in a luxurious manner, rolled up bank deposits approximating $100,000.

Here enters on the scene Jack Rose, Becker's man Friday—Rose, the humble; Rose, the obsequious . . . who, at the last, was to turn and rend the man for whom he had committed blackmail, perjury, and murder.

Rose's real name is Jacob Rosenschwig. He is thirty-seven years old. He was born in Russian Poland, and he seems ashamed of it. . . .

In appearance Rose is one in ten thousand. You need see him only once never to forget him. He has not a hair on his body. His face and head are as smooth and bare as a billiard ball, and from this . . . he gained the sobriquet of "Billiard Ball Jack." The gambling fever was deep in his blood. He would rather gamble than eat—and he often did.

Rosenthal need not be described. He is dead. The murder tore a corner off the underworld and brought to view the rats, the wolves, the preyers, and the preyed scurrying away from the light they so feared.

At that time Herman Rosenthal was running a gambling house on Forty-fifth Street. Rosenthal was a hustler, . . . a moneymaker. Rosenthal the loose-tongued, Rosenthal the babbler. . . .

He had watched Becker's rise closely. . . . He saw in Becker a chance to help himself and at the same time help Becker.

Like the little drops of water, one friction succeeded another between Rosenthal and Becker. Becker made a raid on a crap game during which his press agent, one Charles Plitt, Jr., shot and killed a Negro named Waverly Carter. At the time Becker's money was pretty well tied up . . . so he told Rose to tell Rosenthal that he would like $500 for . . . Plitt's defense.

Rosenthal's refusal . . . caused the relations between the two to buckle, if not break.

Becker knew Rosenthal was dangerous. . . . Late in June, Becker telephoned for Rose to hurry down to the Union Square Hotel where the two were in the habit of meeting almost daily. . . . Becker was much disturbed. He said: "This _____ Rosenthal is . . . trying to prove that I was his partner. He is peddling the story to the newspapers. He is getting really dangerous. He must be stopped."

"That ought to be easy enough," Rose said, not realizing . . . the sinister meaning. . . .

"Jack," responded the policeman, "I want you to go after this fellow Jack Zelig down in the Tombs. We framed him on a charge of carrying a gun. Give him a hundred dollars and tell him that if he wants to save himself you will get him out and that he is to send his gang after Rosenthal."

"What do you mean?" asked Rose, "get them to beat him up?"

"No," answered Becker with scorn . . . "I want him croaked, murdered, his throat cut, dynamited, anything that will take him off the earth. . . . There is no other way of handling the job. *I want you to have him croaked!*"

And as if realizing that the abruptness of his proposition had startled Rose, and fearing that a sufficient cause had not been presented to enlist sympathy in the undertaking, Becker went on. . . .

"Why, Jack, you haven't any idea the kind of man that Rosenthal is. I would be ashamed to tell you the things that he said about you and your wife and your children."

This struck home. Rose . . . agreed that something ought to be done, but he wasn't at all sure as to . . . murder. He temporized, but Becker would have none of it.

So Rose . . . enlisted the support and active cooperation of "Bridgie" Weber and arranged the bail bond for Zelig . . . $10,000. . . .

Rose knew four of Zelig's men . . . Frank Muller, alias "Whitey" Lewis; Harry Horowitz, alias "Gyp the Blood"; Louis Rosenberg, alias "Lefty Louie"; and Frank Ciroficci, alias "Dago Frank." All were mankillers. . . . They knew that he had been responsible for getting Zelig out on bail to await trial on a second offense of carrying concealed weapons which, if substantiated, meant imprisonment for fourteen years. They knew, too, that Rose, through Becker, could have the charge vitiated; so they felt grateful for what he had done for their chief and [were] eager to oblige him. . . .

Certainly they would do the job and [be] glad to. But Rose had no stomach for murder and he sought to fight it off. Becker gave him no rest. Once, twice, three times . . . Becker came to him with reproaches. . . .

"Now," he said, "I want some action or it will be worse for everybody. . . . Go after him anywhere . . . any place you find him . . . I'll take care of everybody that's in it. Not a thing will happen."

Two days later, in the first week of July, Becker ordered Rose to meet him at One hundred twenty-fourth Street and Seventh Avenue where the policeman was to raid a . . . crap game. Rose was there and with him came his errand runner . . . Sammy Schepps. Schepps was sent down to Weber's poker room at Forty-second Street and Sixth Avenue to bring Weber and Vallon to the place. Schepps himself was not to be present. He was not trusted with the secrets, and so he had to wait a half a block away—and in that wait lies the cause of Becker being where he is today. . . .

. . . Rose and Schepps drove up to the . . . apartment house where "Dago Frank" and "Lefty Louie" and their wives had been living and told them to hold themselves in readiness for action that night.

Three of them . . . were stationed in front of the Garden Restaurant at Fiftieth Street and Seventh Avenue where Rosenthal and his wife had been trailed. It was three o'clock in the morning. They were ready . . . but . . . Jack Rose's nerve failed him and he came up on the run from his position a block away to inform the gunmen that they were being shadowed by Burns [International Security Services] detectives working for District Attorney Whitman and that . . . there would be no opportunity for a getaway.

"The next day," Rose swore on the witness stand, "I met Becker and he asked me what was the matter with the Rosenthal job. He wanted to know why it had not been pulled off at the Garden Restaurant as planned. I told him about the detectives, and he said: 'Tell them there isn't anything to be scared of. . . . Why, you tell them that they can shoot Rosenthal in front of any policeman and they'll be all right.' . . ."

"On July 13," Rose continued, "Becker telephoned me that Rosenthal had made an affidavit for the morning *[New York]*

World. Becker said he was going to try to prevent its publication, but he didn't know if he could and he said the whole trouble was my fault because of the delay. I told him that I was going to the Sam Paul outing the next day and I would talk with Vallon and Weber, and all the details would be planned. The next day we went to the outing. We all bought the *World*. We read Rosenthal's affidavit and . . . the statement from Whitman down at Newport. Then we knew that it was really serious.

"On Monday afternoon, July 13, Becker got me on the telephone . . . and told me that Jack Sullivan had just told him that Whitman had made good on the *World's* story and . . . that a secret engagement had been made to put Rosenthal before the Grand Jury the next morning. And . . . that Rosenthal had given the names of Abe Hahlo, Dollar John Lang, and Abe the Rebler, three East Side gamblers. These men were to swear that Becker had been in partnership with Rosenthal and that Becker had been getting graft through me."

Rose left the Lafayette Baths about nine to go to the Sam Paul Association when he met Vallon and Sullivan. Rose ordered an automobile and dropped in, with Sullivan, at Madison Square Garden . . . met Becker and attended a prize fight. . . . Rose and Vallon drove to Dora Gilbert's home where they had several drinks. . . . They succeeded in getting from her an affidavit bitterly hostile to Rosenthal. . . .

. . . A roundup of the murderers was begun. . . .

The red car which Rose had hired . . . lost a tire on the trip from Dora Gilbert's apartment to Tom Sharkey's saloon. So the first thing that Rose did when he arrived there was to telephone to the Cafe Boulevard for Libby and Shapiro's car—the gray murder car, No. 41313.

Here the details were supplied from Rose's narrative:

"Vallon, Schepps, and myself got in. The car was driven by Willie Shapiro. We went up to the Seventh Avenue place where 'Dago Frank' had moved. . . . When we got in front of the house I sent Schepps to ring the bell. A head popped out of the window, and I recognized 'Dago Frank.' He came downstairs and got in, and I asked him where the rest of the boys were, and he told me they had gone ahead.

"We drove down to Forty-third Street and Sixth Avenue. There, in front of the poker room, stood 'Bridgie' Weber, 'Lefty,' 'Whitey,' and 'Gyp.' We all went upstairs. Weber told the . . . waiter to bring us something to eat and drink . . . but I didn't seem to have any appetite. After giving the order, Weber went out. We knew where he had gone and why. He had gone to find Herman Rosenthal and then he was coming back to tell us where he was.

"I found myself hoping that Weber wouldn't locate him. . . . I thought of his wife and how she was worrying every day about Herman, and it broke me all up.

"Just as I was trying to think of some way to stall it off Weber came rushing back and leaned over the table and whispered, 'Rosenthal is at the Metropole now.'

"Even if I had wanted to, before I could say a word, everybody got up and went out. . . . Schepps started to, but I asked him to wait with me."

That Monday night there had been a heavy feeling about Mrs. Rosenthal's heart and she sought to dissuade her husband from leaving. "Don't go out, Herman," she said. "I'm dreadfully worried. . . . Everybody tells me you're in great danger. So stay at home with me at least tonight."

He was a marked man. Everyone in that neighborhood expected that those he had attacked would square matters with him. He passed a group of gamblers . . . and they stopped and told him that he had been the sole topic of conversation and that if he was [sic] a wise man he would go home.

With a cheery "Good night," which, if it were assumed, did not show it, Rosenthal went on. It was then about one o'clock. He entered the restaurant.

The first man he saw there . . . was "Bridgie" Weber. Then he lost sight of him, for a good reason. . . .

Rosenthal talked as he always did of his grievances. So filled was he with this subject that he had become a nuisance to his friends. Twice he left his table, once to . . . speak to a friend . . . and the other time to go purchase some newspapers. . . .

It has never been established whether Rosenthal was sent to or walked to his fate. . . . He had returned to his table and thrown the newspapers down and said in a tone of pride: "That's what the newspapers think of me. Look at that!" and he showed his companions his story . . . on the front page.

Then, refusing another drink and saying that he promised his wife to be home early, Rosenthal threw a dollar down on the table . . . and started out. Some think that just at this time it was that a stranger approached him and said: "Herman, somebody wants to see you outside."

Rosenthal passed through the . . . door and, as his foot touched the pavement, four shots rang out. Four men had been standing on the sidewalk. . . . As Rosenthal emerged they acted in unison. The right arms of three of them snapped up, the left arm of one, and as the pistols spoke Rosenthal toppled forward. . . . As he was falling, the left-handed man pulled his trigger again and sent a bullet crashing into the top of the victim's head. The impact was so powerful that the body turned half around and fell on its side and the eyes stared straight up at the brilliant arc lights, the brows set in an expression of bewilderment, with the mouth parted in a fearful grin. There was a jagged hole in the left cheek, and the dropping jaw and relaxed muscles that let the joints twist horribly showed that medical assistance was unnecessary. . . .

Seven policemen were within five hundred feet of the murder, yet the four men made their flight in safety.

Before the body had settled down the four men had run to a gray car standing . . . in the shadow of the George M. Cohan Theater, . . . clambered aboard, and fled. . . .

One officer had been in the Metropole all the time . . . —Policeman File, who jumped for the street at the flash of the first gun and who stumbled over the body of the dead man, but from whom the murderers were able to escape because of the bystanders who made it dangerous for File to shoot.

"They've murdered Herman Rosenthal!"

This time it was no whisper that spread through the underworld. It was a cry that staggered the city. . . . It stirred the community as never before, for never had a crime of violence given such a direct defiance to law and order.

From an article by Herbert Bayard Swope, reported in the
New York World, October 27, 1912, as quoted in *A Treasury of
Great Reporting,* by Louis L. Snyder and Richard B. Morris, 1949,
pp. 303–311. Copyright © 1949 by Simon and Schuster, Inc.,
a division of Gulf and Western Corporation.
Reprinted by permission of the publisher

LEWIS L. STRAUSS Travels the South as a Shoe Salesman, 1912

A Jew who reads *Men and Decisions* by Lewis L. Strauss (1896-1974) must experience a warm feeling of gratification. A third-generation American, Strauss grew up in West Virginia where there were few Jews. Yet he was an observant Jew and, as he rose to prominence in the political and banking worlds, he avowed his Judaism and gave of himself to the service of his people. He was president of Temple Emanu-El in New York and of the Jewish Agricultural Association (farming was his avocation); he was a leader in the humanitarian work of the Joint Distribution Committee and numerous cultural efforts, both Jewish and general. Strauss is probably best known as the chairman of the Atomic Energy Commission (1953-1958).

One of the chapters in *Men and Decisions* bears a heading in Hebrew of the verse which begins, "Out of the depths I have called Thee" (Psalms 130:1), a striking affirmation of his Jewish identity. In the excerpt which follows, Strauss is observed as a very young man, from the time he became a "drummer"—a travelling shoe salesman in the South.

"As I observed the Sabbath . . . and since most of my customers did not work on Sundays, I had two days each week for study."

IT WAS hard work, physically hard. The tools of the trade were two trunks of sample shoes, each trunk holding eight trays. These had to be unpacked and repacked numbers of times each day. As train schedules were inconvenient and many small communities were served by only one or two stops each day, much of the travelling was done in two-horse hacks hired from a livery stable. . . . Automobiles were uncommon and most of the roads too poor for . . . the early cars.

Getting into the coal mining towns in the narrow valleys of the West Virginia Alleghenies was impossible, however, except by rail and then by walking the crossties between mine commissaries, lugging a case of samples in each hand. . . .

Calling on a merchant for the first time, I used to introduce myself by saying, "I am a son of the vice-president of Fleishman Morris & Company in Richmond, Virginia, and I would like to show you our line of fine shoes." It never occurred to me how this must have sounded until one occasion when I had driven miles, over the sand roads east of the Atlantic Coast Line Railroad, to see a storekeeper in a little settlement. He ran a big commissary, the only one for miles around. When I opened with the introduction, the merchant looked at me and then replied, "Well, sir, I must say that this is a great honor. Imagine it, you, the son of an honest-to-goodness vice-president, coming all the way back into the sticks to see common people like us. Come on up here," he called to his clerks, "come on up here and meet a big man from Richmond." By this time, like Alice in Wonderland, I had shrunk to about two inches and must have shown it. He pulled my leg a little more and then said, "Well, son, I can see you are a new one. Show me your samples." He bought a sizable order and [became] . . . a loyal customer . . . and friend. . . .

There was another customer in a little North Carolina town bisected by the Seaboard Airline Railroad. The "depot" was about three hundred yards from his store. One day the afternoon "cannon-ball express" unloaded my two trunks on a baggage truck and me on the platform, and, as it was late, I could not find a hack to move them to my customer's store. I told my customer of my predicament and said I would get them there in the morning. "How much [are] you going to pay to get them moved?" he asked. I replied that I would pay, perhaps, a dollar. "Then pay me," he said. Whereupon he went to the station and pulled the baggage truck down the street to his store. He was a man at least three times my age. I never forgot that lesson, either.

As I observed the Sabbath by not working on Saturdays, and since most of my customers did not work on Sundays, I had two days each week for study. One of my uncles, who had become wealthy and who lived in New York, would visit the less affluent members of the family in Richmond. On these occasions he would reason with me on the folly of wasting one day out of each week. He assured me that my stubbornness in this respect would doom me to failure in business. By luck, plus a burning desire to prove him wrong, I was able to lead the sales force.

When in small towns where there was no Jewish congregation, I read my prayers alone on the Sabbath and then "read law" in casebooks loaned me by a friend. . . . I also travelled with the Latin classics and enjoyed being able to read them without too great difficulty. This was due to a high school teacher . . . who had made Latin come alive. . . .

In cities where there was a Jewish congregation . . . I attended services, and, on occasion, when the rabbi was away or ill, I was called upon to read. Having had experience as a lay [prayer] reader in Richmond, I was able to discharge this duty to the great satisfaction of my parents. . . .

The main incentive for hard work was to accumulate enough money to be able to go to college and study physics. I had won a scholarship on graduation from high school but for family reasons did not take advantage of it. By 1916, when I was twenty, I had saved about twenty thousand dollars and felt in sight of my goal. That I never did get to college is unfortunately evident enough, though the reason will appear as this account continues. The precise moment my interest in physics began is sharp in my memory.

As a result of a boyhood battle, I had damaged a front tooth and had to be taken to a dentist. In order to keep me amused while he went about making an amalgam or whatever dentists did in those days, he gave me a saucer of mercury. He also had a tuning fork and I found that quite beautiful waves could be produced on the surface of the mercury with the vibrating fork. When the dentist saw what I was doing, he fastened two small wires to the tines of the fork and, setting it vibrating, suggested that the points of the wires be touched to the mercury. There to my astonishment and delight was the first "standing wave" I had ever seen.

As I grew older I read whatever I could find on wave mechanics and radiation. By the time we were studying Millikan's and Gale's *First Course in Physics* in high school, it was already clear that, more than anything else in the universe, the world of physics was the most exciting. The ideal life would be to have enough money to build and equip a laboratory and to work in it to learn the secrets of nature and to expand the frontiers of knowledge. It would cost a lot of money, but, with the overconfidence of youth, that seemed no great obstacle.

Many years later one of the authors of that textbook, Dr. Robert A. Millikan, became a friend. In the intervening years he had won the Nobel Prize for his discoveries in the field of radiation. In the edition of his textbook which I had studied at John Marshall High School, the whole subject of radiation covered only three pages. There was a memorable concluding paragraph:

> J. J. Thompson estimates that enough energy is stored in one gram of hydrogen to raise a million tons through one hundred yards. It is not improbable that it is the transformation of this subatomic energy into heat which is maintaining the temperature of the sun. The most vitally interesting question which the physics of the future has to face is: Is it possible for man to gain control of this tremendous store of subatomic energy and to use it for his own ends? Such a result does not now seem likely or even possible; and yet the transformations which the study of physics has wrought in the world within a hundred years were once just as incredible as this.

The book in which those prophetic words appear was written in 1906. Only the previous year, Albert Einstein, an obscure young patent-office clerk, had published his now famous theorem in a German scientific journal. . . . I still have the textbook, somewhat dog-eared, and, on a weekend at my farm in 1938 [the year 1938 was one year before "fission," four years before the "controlled chain reaction," and seven years before "Hiroshima"], Dr. Millikan came across it in my library and left a note on its flyleaf:

> To Lewis L. Strauss. This was my first attempt [1906] to get across a bit of the history and the method of science. . . .
>
> Robert A. Millikan
>
> 1938

The Great War had begun in 1914, with the German invasion of Belgium, and had been in progress for nearly two and a half years by the winter of 1916-17. There was little excitement about it in the South where I was at work, although there was some prosperity as a result of it. Cotton prices were good and mules were being bought up at high figures to haul the guns and caissons of the Allied armies. Here and there a few volunteers were joining up to fly for the Royal Air Force or to drive ambulances for the Red Cross. It seemed very far away to me.

There was one aspect of the war, however, of which we were generally aware—the plight of Belgium and northern France. Through the newspapers, people were beginning to be familiar with the name of Herbert C. Hoover. . . . His job was to get Americans who had been stranded in Europe by the war back to their homes. Apparently he had done so well at this assignment that, when starvation began in Belgium and northern France, the Ambassador had again turned to Mr. Hoover for help.

There was a story to the effect that, when he set about sending the marooned Americans home, he had advanced his own money for their passage, in many cases relying on good faith to be repaid. He had also engaged his own fortune to get the first shipload of food to be sent to Belgium. Here, obviously, was a man of courage and action, of faith in his fellow men. He had called upon the women of America to collect clothing to be baled and sent to him for distribution to the destitute in the occupied countries. An operation on so large a scale, which today seems a natural reaction to distress in any part of the world, was at that time a pioneering idea. As a result, hundreds of good women, my mother among them, their hearts moved by the suffering of the innocent victims of war, engaged in the collection of warm clothing and blankets from their families and friends. . . .

Early in 1917, the *Richmond Times-Dispatch* carried the item that President Wilson had sent for Mr. Hoover to come to Washington to discuss further relief operations and the management of food production and distribution in the United States so that waste might be eliminated, prices controlled, and production increased. The President's aim was to send more food to England and France. German submarines were increasingly successful in sinking food cargoes. England and France were severely rationing their food, and neither country had any reserves. Reading these reports, my mother was sure that Mr. Hoover was the man to do something about it. That evening she said to me, "When he gets there, why don't you go up and help him?" . . . I had a few weeks on my hands. I also had my savings and could volunteer to work without pay, as the press reported that Mr. Hoover was doing. . . . I took the train to Washington and with some difficulty located Mr. Herbert Clark Hoover in the New Willard Hotel. It was the beginning of an association which, as this is written, has lasted for forty-four years. . . .

A DESPONDENT HEBREW POET
Advises a Younger Colleague, about 1915

In the twelfth century, Judah Alharizi (1170-c.1235), one of the last Spanish Hebrew poets, asked himself despairingly, "For whom do I toil? Who reads my work? Who's interested?"

Six centuries later, Yehudah Leib Gordon (1830-1892), Hebrew poet laureate of his generation, raised this same issue, "Perhaps I am the last of Zion's poets. And, perhaps, you, my readers, are the last of the tribe."

A generation later, a younger colleague, Menachem Mendel Dolitzky (1858-1931), to whom Gordon once wrote, "Here is my pen, rise and take my place!" was assailed by the same doubts. In the new land to which he fled after expulsion from Moscow in 1890, he felt completely isolated. In Russia he had been esteemed by a large, intelligent reading public. Here he was forced to eke out a living by grinding out articles and popular romances in the Yiddish press for an unsophisticated public. In the selection which follows, he advises a younger colleague, Ephraim E. Lisitzky (1885-1962). Lisitzky served many years as a Hebrew educator in New Orleans and is noted for his epic poems about American Indians, about blacks in the South, and about Jewish life in the South; for his Hebrew translations of Shakespeare; and for philosophical essays.

Despite their own frustration and the indifference around them, these men had a deep compulsion not to surrender. Like the prophets of old, they felt, in their very bones, that ultimately the day would come when their toil and suffering would be vindicated.

And come it did, not only in Europe and *Eretz*

Yisrael, but also in the United States. The twentieth century has seen a flowering of Hebrew literature. Today many modern Hebrew books are available in translations. The works of the Hebrew writer, S.Y. Agnon, received the Nobel Prize in 1966.

"The phoenix should be our emblem. . . ."

D OLITZKY had agreed to see me in his hotel the next evening. It was a dilapidated building . . . in the Jewish West Side of Boston. I found him sprawled out on a threadbare couch, tired and depressed after a day spent going from house to house soliciting subscribers for his Yiddish book. He looked grim. It had been a hot summer day; towards evening the air was stifling and humid. Outside, the heat rose from the pavement in waves, streetcars clattered back and forth . . . , wagons and coaches rattled across the cobblestones. Dolitzky's books lay on a bench in the corner . . . ; the gilded letters of his name on the bindings stared at the exhausted poet.

While I struggled to overcome my shyness . . . , he smiled sarcastically:

"Have you read Mendele Mocher Sefarim? You remember the pauper—author, that is to say—who canvasses the rich people in Odessa trying to sell subscriptions to the book he carries around in manuscript form—and how Fishke, the pauper, joins up with the author, and the big-hearted people give Fishke more money as a handout than they give the author for a subscription? I'm that author. Fishke was right: 'Author' is just a newfangled way for saying *schnorer,* beggar. . . .

"You can't reproach a poet for giving up the Muse when he has a wife and children who don't appreciate his heavenly flights when they're hungry. A poet may be willing to sacrifice himself— but he can't allow his family to have empty bellies. . . . Hell is preferable to that."

His harsh voice softened, . . . "You told me you wanted to talk to me. What about?"

I handed him the poem and asked him to . . . give me his opinion of it.

I studied Dolitzky's face intently as he read. . . . My heart was pounding. He looked at me, the same sarcastic smile creasing the corners of his mouth.

"Stop it," he said bitterly. "There's no glory in it. The devil with poetry! . . . You know what happens to Hebrew poets in this country: First stage—Hebrew poet. Second stage—Hebrew teacher, or rather cattle herder, with the children in the role of unwilling cattle. Third stage—you write trashy novels for servant maids and teamsters. You're young, you can get into the university here. Learn an honorable profession that will give you a decent living. Do anything, be anything—peddle candles, be a tailor, a shoemaker—anything but a Hebrew poet in America!"

The street lights outside sifted pallidly through the drawn window shades. Dolitzky did not get up to turn on the gas lamp. . . .

"I came to America. I couldn't endure Russia any more. Pogroms, persecution, oppression, restrictions, humiliation—living in Russia was like living in a snake pit for the Jews. . . . It's very hard leaving a country where you've been born and raised, have studied, have gotten some reputation, and are at home, among your own—the largest and finest Jewish community in the world. Gordon, Yehudah Leib Gordon, helped me make up my mind. *Change your place, change your luck*, he thought. He told me I'd have more scope in a free country. The American Jewish community was young; I would sing new songs there.

"So I took his advice. He wrote me across the ocean: 'Go forth to life and to do battle . . . for the dreams I have dreamt and you shall yet dream.'

" 'Do battle'? With whom? Against whom? What for? In Russia there were people one could fight—respectable enemies. We fought the battle of Enlightenment and Zionism against our Orthodox brethren; but even the most fanatical of them were men of

Title page of first Hebrew-Yiddish poetry book in America. (Jewish Book Annual, *1976, National Jewish Book Council of America)*

stature. . . . They had a tradition to fight for, and you had to respect them for fighting.

"But here in America? If we only had some of those fanatics
and reactionaries from the Old Country here! They at least were
loyal and devout Jews. Here we have a pack of boors, ignora-
muses, whose only thought is to 'make a living.' . . . You can
despise or pity people like that—you can't fight them. And there's
no one to fight with you. The Jewish intellectuals? Heretic Socialists, heroes of *Yom Kippur* and *Tishah Be'av* balls [see selection 8];
or else professional careerists uninterested in their own people.
The few immigrant *maskilim* [intellectuals] are like those lean
stalks of corn in Pharaoh's dream. . . .

"Then, there's nothing to fight *for*. The Enlightenment and
Zionism are disembodied spirits floating in chaos in this country
—in the Old Country they were concrete ideas directly related to
Jewish life. So there you are; in America, the Hebrew poet has no
one to fight against, no one to fight with, and nothing to fight for.
There's no place for him here—he's pushed aside into a corner."

Dolitzky stopped, the words choking in his throat. Silence
filled the room, except for the pendulum of the old clock on the
wall. . . .

"There was one fight I couldn't avoid: making a living. . . . I
tried all kinds of jobs. There was only one that wasn't dishonor-
able—Hebrew teaching.

"There are two kinds of Hebrew teaching in this country . . .
the private kind and the public kind. A Jew rents a room, usually
in a basement, hangs up a gilt sign reading, 'Expert Teacher,
Alphabet, *Maftir, Bar Mitzvah'*—and he's in business as a teacher.
He doesn't make enough out of teaching, so he takes on a few
sidelines, . . . and he puts on his sign: 'Expert *Mohel*, Expert
Marriage Performer, Expert Matchmaker, Expert Evil-Eye Exor-
ciser, Expert Hemorrhoid Remover,' et cetera.

"On the other hand, if you know how and when to pull the
right strings, . . . you can get a job teaching in a Hebrew school.
. . . But if you think the magic name 'Dolitzky' opened doors for

me and got me a decent job in a good school, you're very much mistaken.

". . . I looked through the 'Religious Help Wanted' section of the Yiddish papers. One day I saw something promising and rushed to the address listed. I found several people already there . . . sitting on a bench waiting. . . . I took a seat. As I sat there waiting for my turn in this contest I remembered another contest—where I had won the literary prize given by the B'nai Zion Association in Moscow for my poem, 'On Zion's Hills.' . . .

"I looked around at my competitors: bearded and smooth-faced, lean and fat, they all had one thing in common—they didn't sound like, or look like, men of learning. . . .

"Finally, it was my turn. I walked into the office shamefaced. The chairman of the Education Committee was sitting at the . . . table—a man with a coarse face, pointed beard, a wily look in his eyes.

" 'What's your name, friend?'

" 'Menachem Mendel Dolitzky.'

" 'Russian or Galician?'

" 'Russian.'

" 'Have you ever taught children before?'

" 'Yes!'

" 'Can you read Hebrew?'

" 'They say I can even read the small print.'

" 'They say? Who's they? In America "they say" doesn't mean a thing. . . . Let me hear you read the small print in this prayer book. . . .'

"Finally, I got disgusted with Hebrew teaching and became a Yiddish writer, scribbling fantastic romances for the rabble. It's hack work . . . and a lot of work. There are devotees of the Yiddish novel. . . . But in hard times I have to throw my books into a valise and go out soliciting handouts for them from door to door. . . ."

A knock on the door interrupted Dolitzky. . . . He . . . turned on the gaslight and opened the door. The hotel owner had brought a bundle of just-arrived books—volumes of Dolitzky's collected poetry. . . . He gave me a copy in appreciation of my speech of the night before. Then he continued, somewhat more mildly:

"But don't you listen to me! Write, young man, write! Your poem shows promise. Who knows, maybe there is still hope, we may have fresh young Hebrew poets in this country. Maybe I'm exaggerating American Jewry's defects. Maybe I'm accusing myself, under disguise, when I accuse them. They came to America, oppressed, crushed, impoverished, rootless. They found themselves strangers, everything foreign to them—land, language, way of life. They struggled hard to overcome many obstacles, and that age-old will to live gave them the strength to succeed. It's amazing how they established themselves here: beginning small in petty businesses, ending up big, everywhere in the economy—factories, trades, professions. It's unbelievable!

"True, there are many things wrong with American Jewish life. But still, its very survival is a feat to be commemorated. When the Marranos built a synagogue in Amsterdam they put a phoenix there as an emblem of their resurrection. The phoenix is the immortal bird that arises from its own ashes. The phoenix should be our emblem in America, too. And this material success of ours is certain to precede a victorious conquest of the spirit. That's the way it was with every Jewish settlement—Babylon, Persia, France, Germany, Poland, and Russia—they all began the way American Jewry did, and we'll achieve a spiritual renaissance such as they achieved."

The tears came to his eyes.

"We were the first. We came too early, when the material conquests of the American Jews were still in progress. . . . And we came too late in life, in middle age, lacking youthful enthusiasm and vigor and faith in victory. We gave up with the excuse that there was nothing to fight against, with, or for. We isolated ourselves in a *maskilic* unworldly corner. . . . However, it was a sacred corner. We preserved in it the sacred Hebrew banner we had brought from the Old Country. This sacred banner we now commit to you, the youth, to your keeping. Y.L. Gordon's charge is now addressed to you: *You who go into life—go and make battle!* You will win no easy victory—a difficult struggle lies ahead. And when you are triumphant, do not forget us—the guardians of the Hebrew banner—and do not despise us—the forerunners—do not despise us or deprecate the sorrow of our solitude and the humiliation of our defeat! A little understanding—understanding and forgiveness."

From *In the Grip of Cross Currents*
by Ephraim E. Lisitzky, 1959, pp. 173-179.
Reprinted by permission of the publisher,
Bloch Publishing Company

CYRUS ADLER Celebrates the Completion of the New Translation of the Holy Scriptures, 1917

On *Rosh Hashanah* in 444 B.C.E., in a wide open square in Jerusalem, Ezra the Scribe and Nehemiah, the governor of Judea, surrounded by priests and notables, read the *Torah* to a large gathering of Jews who had returned from the exile in Babylon. They read the text with great feeling; the Levites circulated among the people, interpreting the reading so that the content (Nehemiah 8) would be fully understood.

Helping Jews better understand the *Torah* has been an ongoing concern of Jewish spiritual leaders throughout Jewish history. In the New World, men like Rabbi Isaac Leeser (1806-1868) translated the Scriptures for his generation. But the task was too important and too vast to be entrusted to a single individual. It required a select group of acknowledged scholars representing the different ideologies of American Jewry. The idea of an authoritative translation, acceptable to the diverse denominations in English-speaking Jewry, was launched in 1892 under the aegis of the Jewish Publication Society and was realized *erev Rosh Hashanah,* 1917. The negotiations and the difficulties encountered in the project are described in the preface to that new translation.

In the selection which follows, Cyrus Adler (1863-1940) recalls how he overcame some of the barriers to ultimate success.

*". . . If we only disagree on two points, we
certainly must reach an agreement."*

IN 1908-09 the long-discussed project of a new translation of
the Hebrew Scriptures under the auspices of the Jewish Publication Society of America took form.

Dr. David Philipson, of the Hebrew Union College, and I, old
friends and fellow students at Johns Hopkins University in our
younger years, always maintained happy relations, but there
seemed to be some difficulty about making this project one that
would represent all the Jews, since the Central Conference of
American Rabbis had felt that the translation should emanate
from a rabbinical body and had already made plans to this end.
I wrote to Dr. Philipson and asked him whether, if he were planning to come East, he would call on me in Washington, which he
did. I think that he and his colleagues had pretty well made up
their minds to have a separate project. We sat down in my little
study . . . and talked it over without reaching a definite conclusion. I suddenly conceived the idea of a mechanical device.
I said to him: "Philipson, suppose that I get a long sheet of paper
and divide it in two. Let us put down all the points on which we
agree and all the points on which we do not." He assented, and
it finally turned out that we agreed on nine points and disagreed
on two, and he was generous enough to say: "Well, if we only
disagree on two points, we certainly must reach an agreement."
While there were many more formal discussions in regard to the
production of the Bible, it was on that afternoon in Washington
that the matter was really settled.

My own part was the rather difficult one of Chairman of the
Board of Editors. The company was made up of three men chosen
by the Publication Society: Solomon Schechter, Joseph Jacobs,
and myself; and three chosen by the Central Conference of
American Rabbis: Kaufmann Kohler, David Philipson, and Samuel Schulman. These six chose as the seventh member of the
Board, Max L. Margolis, a distinguished biblical scholar . . . who

The 1917 Bible Translation Committee: (left to right) Dr. Samuel Shulman, Dr. David Philipson, Dr. Max Margolis, Dr. Solomon Schechter, Dr. Kaufmann Kohler, Dr. Joseph Jacobs, and Dr. Cyrus Adler. (Jewish Publication Society of America)

was named Secretary and Editor-in-Chief. The Board met at first in a rather strained atmosphere. Margolis had, a couple of years before, left the Hebrew Union College after a serious difference of opinion between himself, Kohler, and most of the Governors of the College, amongst whom Philipson was prominent. This attitude of strain soon relaxed and, in the course of the seven years the Board sat together, clashes became less frequent, and it was in a spirit of thankfulness to God that we completed these labors. Although here and there a rendering crept in, by vote, which I thought was unhappy, on the whole I felt that a distinct contribution had been made to the interpretation of the Scriptures. The meetings of this Board usually lasted for three weeks and were held in Philadelphia at the Dropsie College, in New York at the Jewish Theological Seminary, several in Atlantic City in the summertime, and one in Cincinnati at the Hebrew Union College.

My wife and I devised various forms of entertainment for our colleagues—a reception, dinners, and the opera—and once we ventured upon a frivolity in the shape of a revue. The grave and reverend gentlemen were much absorbed by the current edition of the Ziegfeld Follies. Opera glasses were in constant use, and, after the show was over, one gentleman astonished us by saying: "I never knew that so many girls were vaccinated on their legs."

One story that stands out in my mind was a quip of Dr. Schechter's. Dr. Kohler was a native of Furth in Bavaria. Kohler told us at luncheon one day that, during the many years the Prince Regent was insane and in an asylum, prayers for his recovery were regularly said in every church and synagogue, only not in Furth. "Well," said Dr. Schechter, "perhaps in Furth insanity is not considered a disease."

The last meeting of the Board was held on November 3, 1915. The whole question of the final manuscript, typography, proofreading occupied quite a period of years. I think that every member of the Board read the proof four times, and Miss Henrietta Szold, who was the Secretary of the Publication Committee, told me that she had read it twelve times. Strangely enough, we had the work printed in Chicago, which also made difficulties, but we found that at that time the best printing establishment for thin paper was located in Chicago. . . . All these steps had been taken, the plates had been made, in fact two sets of plates, and a small advance edition was actually printed.

On Monday evening, January 22, 1917, the Publication Society celebrated the completion of the . . . translation of the Bible by giving a dinner at the Hotel Astor in New York. It was a very interesting and noteworthy occasion, but a strange thing happened. While we were seated at the table, Rabbi Charles I. Hoffman, of Newark, discovered two misplaced lines in the first chapter of the *Book of Isaiah*. Of course there was consternation among us and, since each person present had been given a copy of the Bible, as a souvenir at the dinner, we asked them all to return them and finally had the plates corrected. It seems that a printer's boy had dropped a page of type and covered up the fact. He had the whole page reset. . . . But it was very strange that Rabbi Hoffman, with his eagle eye, and possibly because his middle name is Isaiah, should have discovered this error in a few minutes.

I allowed myself one personal touch in this Bible. The Introduction was written in sections by five of the original company that survived. I was to put it into final form and [I] completed this, the last part of the task, on September 27, 1917. My wife and I had been married on September 27 and it happened that year to coincide with my birthday according to the Jewish calendar, the day before the Jewish New Year. So the Introduction bears the date, September 27. Someone said that the only way in which a modern literary student could be certain of immortality was to have his name connected with the Bible or Shakespeare.

From *I Have Considered the Days*, by Cyrus Adler, 1941, pp. 287-291. Reprinted by permission of the publisher, the Jewish Publication Society of America

A JOURNALIST Relates
Woodrow Wilson's Attitude
toward Jews and Judaism, 1911–1917

Herman Bernstein (1876-1935) was a man of many talents. Russian-born, he arrived in the United States at 17 and eventually became an illustrious journalist in English and in Yiddish.

Bernstein served as correspondent for the leading New York dailies: *The Times, World, Sun,* and *American.* In 1914, he founded and edited a leading Yiddish daily, *Der Tog (The Day),* and edited the *Jewish Daily Bulletin,* the *Jewish Tribune,* and the *American Hebrew.* In the literary world, he is known as a translator of Russian classics and the author of a number of novels on Jewish themes. He achieved national prominence as one of the first to expose the anti-Semitic canards of Henry Ford in the *Dearborn Independent.* In the early thirties, he served as American minister to Albania.

But Bernstein is best remembered as a roving world reporter and correspondent (1909-1924). "I have met practically every outstanding figure of my time," he wrote. "Among them were 'apostles of peace' and 'leaders of unrest'." He reported his interviews with world celebrities. Later he selected the outstanding personalities and included them in a book entitled *Celebrities of Our Time.* Among them were novelist Leo Tolstoy, who was idolized by the Russians; Alexander Kerensky, leader of the revolution which overthrew the czar; Leon Trotsky, who, together with Lenin, overthrew the Kerensky government and turned Russia into a communist state; Pope Benedict XV; George Bernard Shaw, the celebrated British critic and dramatist; Chaim Weizmann; Albert Einstein; and numerous others. The following reflections on President Woodrow Wilson are excerpted from his book, *Celebrities of Our Time.*

"Wherever injustice is done, . . . the moral force of America must be there to defend those who are wronged or oppressed."

I SAW President Wilson in the Hotel Crillon, in Paris, on the day before he returned to America. I heard him speak to a group of American correspondents about the peace treaty. He was still inspired. . . . He realized that the peace treaty was not a perfect document, but . . . the best that could have been secured under the circumstances. . . .

I shall never forget his brief answer to one of the correspondents who asked him whether he believed that America should concern herself with all the troubles of the world.

"Wherever injustice is done, whether it be done to a large group or to a small group, the moral force of America must be there to defend those who are wronged or oppressed."

When the Russian passport question [part of the literacy test; aimed chiefly against the large influx of Jewish immigrants from Russia] began to stir the sense of justice of the American people . . . Wilson delivered an address that was the most inspiring and most important contribution to the cause of equal rights for all American citizens. In that famous speech he said:

"There lies a principle back of our life. America is not a mere body of traders; it is a body of free men. Our greatness is built upon our freedom—is moral, not material. We . . . have a deep passion for the rights of man. Principles lie back of our action. America would be inconceivable without them. . . .

"Here is a great body of our Jewish fellow citizens from whom have sprung men of genius in every walk of our very life; men who have become part of the very stuff of America. . . . They are not Jews in America; they are American citizens. . . . We speak for them as for representatives and champions of principles which underlie the very structure of our government. They have suddenly become representatives of us all. By our actions for them shall be tested our sincerity, our genuineness, the reality of principle among us."

. . . In September, 1911, when Woodrow Wilson was a candidate for the presidency, I had the privilege to introduce him at the National Arts Club to . . . about one hundred journalists and editors of foreign language newspapers. . . . Woodrow Wilson said on that occasion:

"I close as I began, by a very respectful protest against calling yourselves foreign editors or anything with the word foreign in it. Your newspapers and magazines are published in languages which are not the general language of America, . . . but at this stage of the melting-pot process every language in which you print a paper is largely used in the United States and is used for the conveyance of American ideas. Now, I would just as well Americanize a language as Americanize an individual, and I welcome the process by which you are Americanizing other foreign languages as the rest of us have Americanized English or, speaking as someone wittily said, the 'English Slanguage.' All my interest is that you shouldn't regard the language in which you print your periodicals as a foreign language when printed in America for the conveyance of American thinking. . . ."

In July, 1914, President Wilson . . . made the following statement . . . at the dedication of the American University: ". . . Scholarship has usually been most fruitful when associated with religion, and scholarship has never, so far as I can at this moment recall, been associated with any religion except the religion of Jesus Christ."

I wrote him a note inquiring whether he was quoted correctly in the press, adding: "I feel quite certain that you know that true scholarship has ever been and is now the very essence and foundation of Judaism, the religion which gave birth to Christianity. It seems to me that it would, therefore, be unfair to exclude Judaism from the religions with which scholarship has been intimately associated."

On July 9th, President Wilson made public the following letter addressed to me: "I am sorry that there should have been any unfair implication in what I said . . . last week. You may be sure that there was nothing of the kind in my mind, for there certainly is nothing in my thought that would discriminate . . . against Judaism.

"I find that one of the risks and penalties of extemporaneous speaking is that you do not stop to consider the whole field but address yourself merely to the matter directly in hand. . . ."

I remember how deeply he was moved when I related to him the suffering of the people in Palestine during the early stages of the war [World War I] when they needed food and medicines. . . . The Jewish Relief Committee had made vain efforts to secure a boat to send food supplies and medicines. At the request of Dr. [Judah L.] Magnes of the Relief Committee [see selection 27], I took the matter up with the big-hearted, fair-minded Secretary of the Navy, Josephus Daniels, who was sympathetically inclined to help the suffering people of the Holy Land—Jews, Christians, and Moslems—but he feared that it would be impossible to send . . . a government boat, as that would establish a precedent, and other nations might ask for the same. . . .

I then called on President Wilson and familiarized him with the tragic situation. . . . President Wilson was moved to tears. Then he said: "It may be that an American ship will go in that direction before long. Ask Secretary Daniels to let you know when such a ship will start for the Mediterranean, and he will arrange to have space for food supplies and medicines to be shipped to the suffering people in the Holy Land."

Within two weeks I received a telegram from Secretary Daniels notifying me that the *Vulcan* was starting for the Orient and that the Relief Committee would have space for one hundred tons of food . . . and medicines. . . .

I met Woodrow Wilson many times, both as Governor to New Jersey and as President of the United States.

Discussing the literacy test for immigrants, he said to me one day: "This is an unfair and unjust test for immigrants. Criminals and charlatans . . . will not be barred by the literacy test. They can all read and write. But many . . . who come here to flee religious or political persecution, who have been denied the opportunity to acquire the knowledge of reading and writing, would be barred from America . . . even though they are honest and hard-working . . . eager to adapt themselves to American standards of life. . . ."

The following is . . . characteristic . . . :

The White House, Washington,
Shadow Lawn, September 20, 1916

My Dear Mr. Bernstein,

Your plan for a special issue of your magazine has interested me very much, and I avail myself of the opportunity to express my deep interest in the work you are doing for the Jews of America. I hope that they feel . . . that America is a real home in which all forces work together for justice. . . . I need not assure you or them of my genuine interest in my fellow citizens of Hebrew extraction. No man who knows the history of America, or, indeed, of the world, could fail to appreciate their notable contributions to industry, philanthropy, intellectual development, and political liberty.

Cordially and sincerely yours,
Woodrow Wilson

From *Celebrities of Our Time*, by Herman Bernstein,
Hutchinson & Co., London, pp. 307-314

ALEXANDER M. DUSHKIN
Acclaims Samson Benderly's
Contribution to American Jewish
Education, 1910–1920

Jewish education was a forlorn field when the *kehilah* brought Samson Benderly to New York. Born in Safed, Palestine, in 1876, the dynamic Benderly had already achieved remarkable results in Baltimore where he had modernized and Hebraized the school of the Hebrew Education Society.

In New York he immediately started to recruit a new type of Jewish teacher—a college-trained young individual with vision and enthusiasm. Those teachers received special preparation that included Jewish studies at the Teachers Institute of the Jewish Theological Seminary and graduate degrees in education at Columbia University. The men and women he drew into the field were to become national leaders and to influence the entire course of Jewish education in America. Among them was the late Alexander M. Dushkin whose account of some of Benderly's activity is reproduced here.

Many of the techniques and devices introduced by Benderly are taken for granted today, but they were radical innovations in his time. His achievements were lasting. He aroused the community to the need for organizing and modernizing Jewish teaching, made Jewish education into a profession, and trained leaders to carry it on.

"... We were essentially teaching one subject — Judaism!"

I WENT to my interview with Benderly with much hesitation. . . . Dr. Benderly impressed me as a person combining grandiloquent fantasy with realistic engineering. Despite my skeptical approach, I was overwhelmed by his impassioned, urgent optimism as well as by his reasonable analysis of the tasks ahead. His was an attractive, new approach to the forlorn field of Jewish education—a social-engineering approach. . . .

Pragmatically stated, Benderly's plan was "to improve the old and to initiate the new." To improve the old, he proposed to work with a select group of East European educators in the larger *Talmud Torahs* and Hebrew schools. To initiate the new, he needed us young men and women from American colleges. For us, he outlined his threefold plan for "training on the job": (a) to employ us immediately as teachers in model schools . . . and to give us pedagogic supervision and guidance . . . ; (b) to enable us to pursue graduate studies in education toward M.A. and Ph.D. degrees at Teachers College, Columbia University; and (c) to arrange for us special courses in Judaic studies at the Teachers Institute of the Jewish Theological Seminary. . . .

My initial assignment was as teacher in his first model Hebrew preparatory school at the YMHA. Others . . . were assigned to his three other Hebrew preparatory schools or else to the school of the Hebrew Orphan Asylum. . . .

. . . Organizationally, Benderly sought to create a type of school which would provide as intensive a Jewish education as possible . . . to the American Jewish child who attended public school. . . . Each of us was, therefore, to teach four classes, every class receiving six hours of instruction weekly, one afternoon during the week, and on Saturday and Sunday mornings or afternoons. Benderly was experimenting with an "intermittent" school schedule, less demanding than the *Talmud Torah*, more intensive than the Sunday school . . . the forerunner of most of the schedules developed later by congregational Hebrew schools in the United States.

In content, the curriculum of his model schools consisted of the Hebrew language, Bible, and selections from modern Hebrew literature, all taught by the "natural method" (*Ivrit b'Ivrit* [Hebrew in Hebrew]) through specially prepared children's textbooks. Jewish history was taught in English. . . . Music, arts and crafts, dance, and drama . . . and a variety of extracurricular activities were encouraged.

Methodologically, we were then beginning to struggle with the pedagogic classroom problems . . . which have been troubling the modern Jewish educators from that day to this. . . . Benderly was the first to publish Hebrew "movable letters" and flash cards, and he experimented with a variety of Hebrew texts. However, we also had to deal with the principle of function and exercise of a language which, outside of Palestine, was then confined almost entirely to . . . the synagogue. . . . In teaching Bible in Hebrew —which Benderly used to characterize as "teaching the dictionary"—we sought to overcome the insuperable difficulties of content and language, even in the special, abbreviated children's versions by Bialik and others. We attempted the teaching of small "units," with introductory discussions in English of the central ideas. . . . We made preliminary explanations and pupil "dictionaries" of difficult words and phrases; we dramatized the unit in the classroom; we had the children memorize significant biblical phrases. . . . In general, our effort was to "humanize" the Bible for the children.

In teaching Jewish history, we lectured in English with visual aids; adequate history textbooks and other reading aids did not exist then. I became rather expert in "splicing" bits of history films, obtained from whatever sources were then available, and in rearranging pictures, cut out from sundry books on the Bible and Jewish history, for use in overhead projection. . . . In our teaching about Palestine, Jewish festivals, customs, and current events, we used school newspapers, assembly dramatizations, arts and crafts, and the like. Benderly kept impressing on us that, in all our teaching, we were essentially teaching one subject—Judaism!

There was the quality of the *chasidic rebbe* in Benderly, and he molded us into a camaraderie of believers. We considered ourselves a band of pioneers who were "hastening the footsteps of the Messiah." . . .

Benderly's professional career in America was itself an impressive personal "act of faith." Upon his graduation from medical school, he was called upon to decide between a brilliant medical career and his "infatuation" with lowly Jewish education. He chose the latter, and that was the faith he imparted to us. . . .

Our Judaic studies at the Jewish Theological Seminary—with Mordecai M. Kaplan, Israel Friedlaender, Moshe Levin, and others —were carried on during evenings after the day's work was done, and more intensively during the summer. . . . Our Jewish training could be characterized as Hebraic-national in the Ahad Ha-Am spirit of cultural Zionism and religious in the neo-Chasidic-Conservative-Reconstructionist spirit. All our teachers were cultural Zionists and belonged to the "historic school" of Jewish scholarship.

Kaplan, Friedlaender, and [Judah L.] Magnes taught us the ethnic community approach to Judaism. . . . Kaplan was the *ma'ayan hamitgabber,* an ever-rushing stream, both destructive and reconstructive. His teachings fitted in with our deep needs as American youth for a new conception of Judaism for our day. His vision of reconstructed Judaism as the civilization of a religiously endowed people was like a "fire in his bones." His provocative, passionate, and positive "message" had in it an element of the prophetic. . . .

Our professional university education was in the Teachers College of Columbia University in the days of John Dewey, William H. Kilpatrick, and Edward L. Thorndike, with their provocative new messages in American education. . . . It was the teachings of the three "greats"—Dewey, Kilpatrick, and Thorndike—at Columbia in those days that remained with me throughout the years. . . .

. . . Benderly took some of us into the Bureau of Jewish Education proper to engage in other experimental ventures: the League of Jewish Youth and the Circle of Jewish Children . . . ; the Jewish Home Institute . . . (for the pedagogic guidance of mothers in teaching their preschool children); research and information services; Hebrew high school classes; publications of . . . educational materials. . . .

Opposition to Benderly came from many sources. The Orthodox rabbis opposed him as an "assimilationist." . . . Conservative rabbis accused him of being a "secularist," and the Reform Jews opposed him as a "nationalist." More compelling were his increasing financial difficulties. Benderly liked to tell the story of his conversation with his friend, the financier Jacob H. Schiff, who was in the habit of talking to him about "Judaism as a faith"—to which he once replied: "The trouble, Mr. Schiff, is that you worry about philosophy and expect me to worry about finances. It would be much better if our roles were reversed."

From "Autobiographical Reflections," by Alexander M. Dushkin,
American Jewish Archives, Vol. 21, No. 2, pp. 118-129.
Reprinted by permission of the American Jewish Archives